A(ZX)103

An Introduction to the Humanities

The Open University

Resource Book

2

This publication forms part of an Open University course A(ZX)103 *An Introduction to the Humanities*. Details of this and other Open University courses can be obtained from the Student Registration and Enquiry Service, The Open University, PO Box 197, Milton Keynes, MK7 6BJ, United Kingdom: tel.+44 (0)870 333 4340, email general-enquiries@open.ac.uk

Alternatively, you may visit the Open University website at http://www.open.ac.uk where you can learn more about the wide range of courses and packs offered at all levels by The Open University

To purchase a selection of Open University course materials visit http://www.open.ac.uk, or contact Open University Worldwide, Michael Young Building, Walton Hall, Milton Keynes MK7 6AA, United Kingdom for a brochure. tel. +44 (0)1908 858785; fax +44 (0)1908 858787; e-mail ouwenq@open.ac.uk

The Open University
Walton Hall, Milton Keynes
MK7 6AA

First published 1997. Second edition 2005.

Copyright © 1997 The Open University

Edited and designed by The Open University.

Typeset by The Open University.

Printed and bound in the United Kingdom by CPI, Bath.

ISBN 0 7492 9661 5

2.1

31612B/a103rb2i2.1

Contents

Section A HISTORY: INTRODUCTION TO HISTORY

A1 Chronology showing key events of the Revolution

1786 August	It is clear that the monarchy is facing bankruptcy, and that reforms both in administration and in tax collection are essential. There would be powerful opposition to such reforms, and there is no obvious way of securing consent to them.
1787 February	The royal government summons an assembly of hand-picked nobles, 'The Assembly of Notables'.
1787 May	The 'Assembly of Notables' refuses to accept the reform programme and is dismissed. It is widely argued that the reform programme can only achieve legitimacy by being presented to an Estates General.
1788 May–July	The *parlements* refuse to register reforms, and are suspended.
1788 August–September	The royal government gives way. It is announced that an Estates General will be summoned for the following May. The former finance minister Necker, popular with all classes, is recalled. The *parlements* are reinstated. Meantime the harvest is disastrous.
1789 Early months	Elections to the Estates General take place, with many debates about how the Estates should meet and vote. All districts are invited to send in formal statements of their grievances (*cahiers de doléances*) for discussion by the Estates General. There are bread riots in Paris and the provinces.
1789 May	The Estates General convenes. Continuing arguments about whether it should meet as one body (which would give the Third Estate a majority) or whether it should vote as three separate estates.
1789 June	The Third Estate, joined by some clerical members, adopts the title 'National Assembly'. Three days later this 'National Assembly' finds itself locked out and takes the Tennis Court Oath, swearing not to disband till France has adopted a formal constitution. The king attends a 'royal session' of the entire Estates General, and appears reluctant to accept the notion of being a constitutional monarch.
1789 July	The National Assembly adopts the title National Constituent Assembly, signifying that its main task is to draw up a constitution. The king dismisses Necker. Already there is agitation and discussion among various social groups in Paris. Bread riots, anger over the dismissal of Necker, rumours that the king plans to use the army to restore his position in full, and an actual armed clash between soldiers and the people of Paris, sets Paris demonstrators off on a search for weapons.

This is the main motive for their successful attack on the Paris fortress of the Bastille. Those Parisians who had the right to vote for the Estates General (bourgeois *and* some artisan elements) form themselves into the Paris Commune and establish a National Guard under the command of the liberal aristocrat, Lafayette. The countryside is pervaded by the 'Great Fear'. There is famine, there are brigands – the peasants, having been encouraged to believe that their grievances were to be met, now fear that they are being attacked by the nobles, and they in turn attack castles and manor houses, wherever possible destroying all records of the feudal dues they owe to the nobles.

1789 August	The National Constituent Assembly, reinforced by some nobles and more clergy, begins the promulgation of a constitution with a preliminary 'Declaration of the rights of man and the citizen'. Intimidated by the direct action of the peasants in the 'Great Fear' it also abolishes all feudal dues.
1789 September	The king summons the Flanders Regiment to Versailles, where, against a background of banquets and loyalist toasts, he announces his reservations about both the decrees abolishing feudalism and the 'Declaration of the rights of man and the citizen'.
1789 October	Women lead processions from various markets to the Paris town hall, and then a vast assemblage of armed citizens sets off for Versailles. The king is intimidated into moving his residence to the Tuileries in Paris. The Assembly shortly follows.
1789 November	Church lands taken over (and steadily made available for purchase – including by peasants).
1790	Throughout the year the Assembly continued its work on the constitution and on the voting system.
1790 June	The Assembly abolishes all ranks, titles, and privileges of the nobility.
1790 July	The Civil Constitution of the Clergy makes the clergy subject to election like all other public officials.
1790 November	The Assembly votes to dismiss forthwith all clerics who do not totally accept the new dispensation and to impose on all clergy an oath of loyalty to the new regime. This provokes bitter divisions throughout the country and there are a number of anti-revolutionary insurrections.
1791 Early months	Though the king appears to be acting as a constitutional monarch he is actually unreconciled to this role.
1791 June	The king attempts to flee the country, leaving behind a denunciation of the new regime, but is stopped at Varennes. The Assembly suspends him but is reluctant to end the monarchy.
1791 July	'The Massacre of Champ de Mars' – petitioners against retaining the monarchy are shot down by the National Guards, under Lafayette.

1791 August	'Declaration of Pillnitz' – the Emperor of Austria and the king of Prussia declare themselves willing to restore the French king to full powers.
1791 September	The king, restored to executive power, accepts the new constitution, and the Assembly is dissolved. Elections (on a franchise which is actually more restricted than that of the Estates General) proceed.
1791 October	The new 'Legislative Assembly' convenes. Punitive decrees are immediately promulgated against priests refusing to take the oath, and *émigrés* (opponents of the Revolution who had fled the country and were constantly plotting a royalist invasion). The king, as was his right under the new constitution, vetoed both of them. Land forfeited by *émigrés* steadily becomes available for purchase (including to peasants).
1792 January	As a result of the slave rebellion in the West Indies beginning in August 1791, there is a sugar shortage: women again led the mobs which surged through Paris.
1792 Early months	For contrasting reasons, different groups in France welcome the idea of foreign war; in particular, revolutionaries, because they believe it will consolidate the Revolution, and the king, because he believes it will lead to foreign powers restoring him to absolute power. Riots throughout France against shortages and high prices.
1792 April	France declares war on Austria. Early defeats for the French forces create fear and suspicion in Paris.
1792 June	The king dismisses his anti-clerical, pro-war, ministers, resulting in the invasion of the Tuileries Palace by 10,000–20,000 armed demonstrators, calling themselves sansculottes (literally, 'without breeches', that is 'wearers of working-class clothes', though many were in fact bourgeois). There was no immediate outcome, but the sansculottes had signalled their arrival as yet another important extra-parliamentary force.
1792 July	Arrival for Fall of Bastille celebrations of large number of provincial National Guards (known as *fédérés*). These join with the various groups of Paris citizens. News reaches Paris that the Austrians have invaded north-east France and that the Duke of Brunswick has threatened Paris with 'exemplary and forever memorable violence'. War and revolution become interlinked as the Assembly authorizes distribution of arms to all citizens.
1792 August	'The Revolution of 10 August': the Paris groups, backed by the *fédérés*, mount a second invasion of the Tuileries; the Assembly, completely overawed, again declares the monarchy suspended, but this time imprisons the King, and declares that a new Convention, based on universal suffrage, will be convened. For the moment the Paris Commune is in charge – as elections to the Convention are taking place, vengeance is wreaked on all the Commune see as enemies. Paranoia is intensified by the news that the Prussians have invaded France.

The 'First Terror' begins, with the guillotine being used for the first time on political prisoners.

1792 September	The Austrians capture Verdun. Prisoners massacred – justified on grounds that a potential 'fifth column' could not be left in the heart of Paris, but condemned by many historians. The citizen armies go forth and secure a first victory at Valmy. The new Convention meets and declares France a republic.
1792 November	The French armies invade the Low Countries, and proceed to sweep eastwards.
1792 December	The king put on trial before the Convention.
1793 January	Execution of Louis XVI.
1793 February	The French Republic declares war on Great Britain. There are food riots in Paris. The raising of 300,000 conscripts is announced.
1793 March	France at war with Spain. Attempted conscription provokes revolts in La Vendée in the west of France, where pro-clerical sentiment is strong. France has again suffered several military setbacks so Committee of Public Safety is established. Attempt to control grain prices through the *maximum*.
1793 May–June	'Federalist' revolts against Paris domination break out in many important provincial centres. The end of May was a time of bitter crisis between the Paris Commune and the leading group in the Convention, known as the Girondins (they came from the Bordeaux area, on the River Gironde). The Girondins resented the pressures from Paris, and had some sympathy with the anti-Paris movements in the provinces. Another Paris insurrection on 31 May and 1 June resulted, on 2 June, in the purge of the Girondins from the Convention. Those known as the Jacobins were now in the ascendant: constitution-making was suddenly speeded up, and a new radical constitution approved; at the same time further radical measures aimed at appeasing the peasants were passed.
1793 August	The *levée en masse* (mass conscription) – conscript army of over one million to be raised in a year. Rebels at Toulon turn the port over to the British.
1793 September	New phase of bread and wage riots. Sansculottes enforce further revolutionary change, Law of Suspects and intensified terror.
1793 October	Lyon surrenders to government forces: terror there. New revolutionary calendar (Year I, etc., new names for months) introduced and then programme of dechristianization.
1793 November	Festival of Reason (designed by David).
1793 December	New centralized 'Revolutionary Government' instituted with power concentrated in the Committee of Public Safety (on which Robespierre, who had joined it in July, was the most powerful figure).

1794 February	Laws providing for the confiscation of lands of political suspects. Robespierre declares: 'If the aim of popular government in peacetime is virtue, then the aim of popular government in a time of revolution is virtue and terror at one and the same time; virtue without which terror is disastrous, terror without which virtue is impotent.' Abolition of slavery.
1794 March	Committee of Public Safety turns against the Parisian popular movements, and their alleged insurrectionist leaders.
1794 March–April	Terror intensifies.
1794 April	Rousseau's ashes moved to Pantheon.
1794 June	Robespierre, praising Rousseau, institutes Festival of the Supreme Being (designed by David).
1794 July	Beginning of reaction against Robespierre. Arrest and execution of Robespierre and his followers.
1794 August	Full reaction against the Terror. Girondins back in power in what is often termed 'the Thermidorean reaction' (after the name of the month). Release of political prisoners. Rise of anti-sansculottes vigilantes, the 'Gilded Youth'.
1794 November	Jacobin club closed.
1794 December	Abolition of the *maximum*. Disastrously cold winter begins.
1795 March	Churches reopen for public worship.
1795 April	Bread riots.
1795 Spring and Summer	Counter-terror of lynchings and hackings to death. Great popular risings for food and the restoration of the constitution of 1793 suppressed.
1795 June	Abolition of use of word 'revolutionary' when referring to government.
1795 August	Victories abroad ensure that royalism is no longer a threat. Believing that stability is the element most required, the Convention approves a new conservative constitution (Constitution of the Year III), setting up a bicameral legislature consisting of the Council of Five Hundred and the Council of Elders.
1795 October	Insurrection against this regime repressed, with the 26-year-old artillery general Bonaparte distinguishing himself.
1795 November	The Directory (a governing body of five) established.
1796 Spring	Serious food shortages. Babeuf conspiracy on behalf of the poor (modelled on the revolt in Ancient Rome – again! – of the Gracchi) suppressed.
1797 March–April	Elections show unpopularity of Directory; Bonaparte continues victorious abroad.
1797 September	Coup establishes 'Second Directory' and annuls election results.

1797 Autumn	'Directorial Terror'.
1799 August	Royalist risings.
1799 October	Return to France of a victorious Bonaparte.
1799 November	Coup establishes the provisional government of three consuls, of whom one is Bonaparte.
1799 December	New constitution. Citizen Bonaparte is 'First Consul'.
1801	German lands on west side of Rhine incorporated into France.
1801 July	Catholic Church restored in full in France.
1802	Napoleon I declared *hereditary* First Consul.
1804 December	Napoleon crowned Emperor of France by the Pope.
1805 December	Napoleon crushes Austrians at Austerlitz.
1806	Napoleon abolishes (Habsburg) Holy Roman Empire of Germans, and sets up the Confederation of the Rhine (of all West German territories) under French Consul.
1806 October	Napoleon crushes the Prussians at Jena.

Primary sources

A2 Calonne's reform programme, 26 August 1786

From W. Doyle (1988) *The Origins of the French Revolution*, 2nd edn, Oxford University Press, p.52.

The disparity, the disaccord, the incoherence of the different parts of the body of the monarchy is the principal of the constitutional vices which enervate its strength and hamper all its organization; ... one cannot destroy any one of them without attacking them all in the principle which has produced them and which perpetuates them; ... it alone influences everything; ... it harms everything, ... it is opposed to all good; ... a kingdom made up of lands with estates, lands without, lands with provincial assemblies, lands of mixed administration, a Kingdom whose provinces are foreign one to another, where multifarious internal barriers separate and divide the subjects of the same sovereign, where certain areas are totally freed from burdens of which others bear the full weight, where the richest class contributes least, where privileges destroy all balance, where it is impossible to have either a constant rule or a common will, is necessarily a very imperfect kingdom, brimming with abuses, and one that it is impossible to govern well; ... in effect the result is that general administration is excessively complicated, public contributions unequally spread, trade hindered by countless restrictions, circulation obstructed in all its branches, agriculture crushed by overwhelming burdens, the state's finances impoverished by excessive costs of recovery, and by variations in their product. Finally, I shall prove that so many abuses, so visible to all eyes, and so justly censured, have only till now resisted a public opinion which condemns them, because nobody has attempted to extirpate their germ, and to dry up the source of all obstacles by establishing a more uniform order.

A3   Petition of the women of the Third Estate to the king, 1 January 1789

From D.G. Levy, H.B. Applewhite and M.D. Johnson (1979), *Women in Revolutionary Paris, 1789–1795*, Urbana, University of Illinois Press, pp.18–21.

Sire,

At a time when the various orders of the state are busy with their interests, when everyone is trying to assert his titles and his rights, when some people are worrying about recalling centuries of servitude and anarchy, when others are making every effort to shake off the last links which still bind them to the imperious remains of the feudal system, women – continual objects of the admiration and scorn of men – women, wouldn't it be possible for them also to make their voices heard amidst this general agitation?

Excluded from the national assemblies by laws too well consolidated for them to hope to break, they do not ask, Sire, for your permission to send their deputies to the Estates General; they know too well how great a role interest would play in an election and how easy it would be for the representatives to impede the freedom of the votes.

We prefer, Sire, to place our cause at your feet; not wishing to obtain anything except from your heart, we address our complaints and confide our miseries to it.

The women of the Third Estate are almost all born without fortune; their education is very neglected or very defective: it consists in their being sent to schools at the house of a teacher who himself does not know the first word of the language he is teaching. They continue going there until they are able to read the service of the Mass in French and Vespers in Latin. Having fulfilled the first duties of religion, they are taught to work; having reached the age of fifteen or sixteen, they can make five or six *sous* a day. If nature has refused them beauty, they get married without dowry to unfortunate artisans, lead aimless, difficult lives stuck away in the provinces, and give birth to children they are incapable of raising. If, on the contrary, they are born pretty, without culture, without principles, without any idea of morals, they become the prey of the first seducer, commit a first sin, come to Paris to bury their shame, end by losing it altogether, and die victims of licentious ways.

Today, when the difficulty of subsisting forces thousands of them to put themselves up for auction, when men find it easier to buy them for a spell than to win them over forever, those whom a happy penchant inclines to virtue, who are consumed by the desire to learn, who feel themselves led by a natural taste, who have overcome the deficiencies of their education and know a little of everything without having learned anything, those, to conclude, whom a haughty soul, a noble heart, a pride of sentiment cause to be called *prudish*, are forced to throw themselves into cloisters where only a modest dowry is required, or forced to hire themselves out when they do not have enough courage, enough heroism to share the generous devotion of the daughters of Vincent de Paul.

Also, several, solely because they are born girls, are disdained by their parents, who refuse to set them up, preferring to concentrate their fortune on the head of a son whom they designate to carry on their name in the capital; for it is good that Your Majesty understands that we also have names to keep up. Or, if old age finds them spinsters, they spend it in tears and see themselves the object of the scorn of their nearest relatives.

To prevent so many ills, Sire, we ask that men not be allowed, under any pretext, to exercise trades that are the prerogative of women – such as seamstress, embroiderer, fashion merchant, etc., etc.; if we are left at least with the needle and the spindle, we promise never to handle the compass or the square.

We ask, Sire, that your benevolence provide us with the means of putting to use the talents with which nature has furnished us, notwithstanding the impediments which are forever being placed on our education.

May you assign us positions, which we alone will be able to fill, which we will occupy only after having passed a strict examination, after trustworthy inquiries concerning the purity of our morals.

We ask to be enlightened, to have work, not in order to usurp men's authority, but in order to be better esteemed by them, so that we might have the means of living out of the way of misfortune and so that poverty does not force the weakest among us, who are blinded by luxury and swept along by example, to join the crowd of unfortunate beings who overpopulate the streets, and whose debauched audacity is a disgrace to our sex and to the men who keep them company.

We would want this class of women to wear a mark of identification. Today, when they go so far as to adopt the modesty of our dress, when they mingle everywhere in all kinds of clothing, we often find ourselves taken for them; some men are mistaken and make us blush because of their scorn. It would be necessary that under pain of having to work in the public workshops for the benefit of the poor (it is known that work is the greatest punishment that can be inflicted on them), they never be able to remove this mark ... However, it occurs to us that the empire of fashion would be destroyed and one would run the risk of seeing many too many women dressed in the same color.

We implore you, Sire, to set up free schools where we could learn our language on the basis of principles, religion and ethics. May one and the other be offered to us in all their grandeur, entirely stripped of the petty applications which attenuate their majesty; may our hearts be formed there; may we be taught above all to practice the virtues of our sex; gentleness, modesty, patience, charity; as for the arts that please, women can learn them without teachers. Sciences? ... they serve only to inspire us with a stupid pride, lead us to pedantry, go against the decrees of nature, make of us mixed beings who are rarely faithful wives and still more rarely good mothers of families.

We ask to come out of the state of ignorance, to be able to give our children a sound and reasonable education so as to make of them subjects worthy of serving you. We will teach them to cherish the beautiful name of Frenchmen; we will transmit to them the love we have for Your Majesty, for we are willing to leave valour and genius to men, but we will challenge them over their dangerous and previous gift of sensitivity; we defy them to love you better than we; they run to Versailles, most of them, for their interests, and when we, Sire, see you there, with difficulty and with pounding hearts, and are able to gaze for an instant upon your August Person, tears flow from our eyes. The idea of Majesty, of Sovereign, vanished, and we see in you only a tender Father, to whom we would sacrifice our lives a thousand times.

A4 Declaration of the rights of man and the citizen, August 1789

From D.G. Wright (1974) *Revolution and Terror in France, 1789–1795,* Longman, pp.107–10.

The representatives of the French people, sitting in the National Assembly considering that ignorance of, neglect of, and contempt for the rights of man are the sole causes of public misfortune and the corruption of governments, have resolved to set out in a solemn declaration the natural, inalienable and sacred rights of man, in order that this declaration, constantly before all members of the civic body, will constantly remind them of their rights and duties, in order that acts of legislative and executive power can be frequently compared with the purpose of every political institution, thus making them more respected; in order that the demands of the citizens, henceforth founded on simple and irrefutable principles, will always tend towards the maintenance of the constitution and the happiness of everyone.

Consequently the National Assembly recognises and declares, in the presence of, and under the auspices of, the Supreme Being, the following rights of man and of the citizen:

(i) Men are born and remain free and equal in rights. Social distinctions can only be founded on communal utility.

(ii) The purpose of all political associations is the preservation of the natural and imprescriptible rights of man. These rights are liberty, property, security and resistance to oppression.

(iii) The principle of all sovereignty emanates essentially from the nation. No group of men, no individual, can exercise any authority which does not specifically emanate from it.

(iv) Liberty consists in being able to do whatever does not harm others. Hence the exercise of the natural rights of every man is limited only by the need for other members of society to exercise the same rights. These limits can only be determined by the law.

(v) The law only has the right to prohibit actions harmful to society. What is not prohibited by law cannot be forbidden, and nobody can be forced to do what the law does not require.

(vi) The law is the expression of the general will. All citizens have the right to take part personally or through their representatives, in the making of the law. It should be the same for everyone, whether it protects or punishes. All citizens, being equal in the eyes of the law, are equally admissible to all honours, offices and public employment, according to their capacity and without any distinction other than those of their integrity and talents.

(vii) A man can only be accused, arrested or detained in cases determined by law, and according to the procedure it requires. Those who solicit, encourage, execute, or cause to be executed, arbitrary orders must be punished, but every citizen called upon or arrested in the name of the law must obey instantly; resistance renders him culpable.

(viii) The law must only require punishments that are strictly and evidently necessary, and a person can only be punished according to an established law passed before the offence and legally applied.

(ix) Every man being presumed innocent until he has been declared guilty, if it is necessary to arrest him, all severity beyond what is necessary to secure his arrest shall be severely punished by law.

(x) No man ought to be uneasy about his opinions, even his religious beliefs, provided that their manifestation does not interfere with the public order established by the law.

(xi)   The free communication of thought and opinion is one of the most precious rights of man: every citizen can therefore talk, write and publish freely, except that he is responsible for abuses of this liberty in cases determined by the law.

(xii)   The guaranteeing of the rights of man and the citizen requires a public force: this force is therefore established for everybody's advantage and not for the particular benefit of the persons who are entrusted with it.

(xiii) A common contribution is necessary for the maintenance of the public force and for administrative expenses; it must be equally apportioned between all citizens, according to their means.

(xiv)   All citizens have the right, personally, or by means of their representatives, to have demonstrated to them the necessity of public taxes, so that they can consent freely to them, can check how they are used, and can determine the shares to be paid, their assessment, collection and duration.

(xv)   The community has the right to hold accountable every public official in its administration.

(xvi)   Every society which has no assured guarantee of rights, nor a separation of powers, does not possess a constitution.

(xvii) Property being a sacred and inviolable right, nobody can be deprived of it, except when the public interest, legally defined, evidently requires it, and then on condition there is just compensation in advance.

A5 Extracts from a letter from Marquis de Ferrières to M. de Fabreuil, Versailles, 7 August 1789

From Herve Carré (ed.) (1932) *Marquis de Ferrières: Correspondance Inédite*, Paris, Librairé Armand Colin, pp.113–15 (extracts translated by Arthur Marwick).

Sir, the sitting on the evening of Tuesday 4 August was the most memorable sitting which has ever taken place in any nation. It was redolent of the noble enthusiasm of the Frenchman. It showed to the entire universe how great is his generosity and the sacrifices of which he is capable, to which he is commanded by honour, love of the good, and patriotic heroism ...

The dukes of Aiguillon and of Châtelet proposed that, from that moment, the Nobility and the Clergy should give up their financial privileges ...

The unhappy circumstances in which the nobility find themselves, the general insurrection against them in all parts ... more than one-hundred-and-fifty castles burned to the ground; their feudal titles sought out in a kind of fury, then burned; the impossibility of resisting the torrents of the Revolution, the misfortunes that follow any resistance however futile; the ruin of the most beautiful kingdom in Europe, prey to anarchy and devastation; but, more than all that, that love of one's country innate in the heart of the Frenchman, love which is an absolute duty for the noble, obliged by state and by honour, to devote his possessions, and his life to the king, and to the Nation; everything prescribed the conduct we must follow; there is only one general movement. The Clergy, the Nobility rose up and supported every motion proposed. The flattering expressions of gratitude were prodigious. But it was a moment of patriotic drunkenness.

Different motions succeeded each other with rapidity. One demanded free justice; and the commons hastened to applaud it; another proposed reduction in pensions, governorships, courtiers' expenses; it was received with acclamation. The clergy offered to give up their surplice fees. Some went as far as the proscription of holding more than one benefice, and gave up those they had. Deputies from Paris renounced the privileges of the capital, those from Bordeaux, Lyon, Marseilles followed their example; the deputies from the privileged provinces ... came forward in turn to solemnly pronounce, in the name of their provinces, the formal renunciation of all rights, privileges, exemptions and prerogatives, demanding to be assimilated with the other provinces of France. You can imagine the enthusiasm with which such generous renunciation was received. I will make no effort to paint for you the transports of joy; an immense crowd of spectators took part in it; there was shouting, cries of 'Long Live the king!', clapping of hands!

This union of interests, this unity of the whole of France in one single goal (the common advantage of all) which twelve centuries, the same religion, the same language, the long sharing of the same customs had not been able to bring about; which the most powerful and skilful minister had not been able to achieve, after ten years of work and application, found itself established in one moment, and sanctioned for ever.

A6 Extracts from Paul-Philippe Gudin, *Supplement to the Social Contract*, 30 October 1790

From P. Ph. Gudin (1791) *Supplément au Contract Social*, Paris, Chez Maradan et Perlet, pp.3, 21, 97, 121, 194, 200 (extracts translated by Arthur Marwick).

These ideas form a natural supplement to Rousseau's *Social Contract*: a supplement all the more necessary since one ceaselessly searches in that excellent work for fundamental principles without always finding ones which are applicable to the vast kingdom we are concerned with: since Rousseau, the citizen of a tiny republic, had experience only of small States ...

... the profound genius of the author of the *Social Contract* enabled him to identify the characteristic signs of the general will; he has pointed them out to us, they are such that it is impossible to misunderstand them.

Individual will, he said[1] *in its nature tends always to personal preferences and the general will to equality.*

It is not certain, he said further in his treatise on political economy, *that the decision of the people will be an expression of the general will.*

The general will is always for the party favourable to the public interest, that is to say, the most equitable, with the result that it can only be just, to be assured of following the general will.

Equality of rights, justice in everything; here are the signs by which citizens can always tell whether the laws being proposed to them emanate from the general will, or from that of a party which holds a majority of votes.

... the revolution has come, not because the philosophers enunciated truths useful both to rulers and peoples, as the enemies of all good seek to blame them with, and as feeble people whom they upset repeat unendingly; but it has come, on the contrary, because nobody acted upon their proposals for avoiding the revolution which they foresaw ...

If the capitalist is wise, by his expenditure he will cause crafts, commerce, manufacturers and even agriculture to flourish. If he is stupid, he will still make them flourish through his excesses; and his wealth, which he does not know how to use, will soon be dispersed, being shared out and passing into hard-working and industrious hands which will make better use of it ...

In his *Social Contract* one finds all the fundamental principles of society and of liberty; in his *Considerations on the Government of Poland*, all the principles necessary for regenerating this kingdom, and for securing liberty around the throne. He proves that people cannot be happy without being free ...

... in this supplement to the *Social Contract*, I have not always followed Rousseau: the educated reader will easily see where and why I have strayed. He was too severe in his own time, and I am perhaps too indulgent in mine: but I believe him inferior to no one, and superior to most of those who preceded him: Rousseau hoped for nothing from his contemporaries, I have not given up hope on mine.

[1] *Social Contract*, bk2, ch.1.

A7 Extracts from Sebastien Mercier, J.J. Rousseau, considered as one of the first authors of the Revolution, June 1791

From M. Mercier (1791) *De J.J. Rousseau consideré comme l'un des premier auteurs de la révolution*, Paris, Chez Buisson, tome premier, Juin, pp.1–2, 19–20, 159, 165, 167 (extracts translated by Arthur Marwick).

Within a very short period of time, France has lost the writers in whom she justifiably takes such pride ... from the day when death claimed those sovereigns of the literary empire, the star of their reputation has seemed to wane and lose its brightness before posterity ... Among those columns which in France suggested the temple of genius, only one perhaps still stands up to its full height; and on that column there is no one who does not read, or who does not engrave with us the name of J.J. Rousseau ...

... what placed J.J. Rousseau above all the writers of his century was that his eloquence had a moral character, a quality of real and general usefulness ...

... Rousseau ... saw that societies can only exist, or at least prosper, through *public virtue* ...

It was, therefore, with the *public virtue* of Rousseau that the national assembly (after many centuries of barbarity and delirium ...) recreated the natural politics which will travel the world ...

The free and proud genius of the national assembly adopting, despite *satrapism* and *despotism, public virtue,* placed itself above vulgar minds.

A8 Olympe de Gouges, *The Declaration of the Rights of Woman*, 1791

From D.G. Levy, H.B. Applewhite and M.D. Johnson (1979) *Women in Revolutionary Paris, 1789–1795*, Urbana, University of Illinois Press, pp.87–96.

To the Queen: Madame,

Little suited to the language one holds to with kings, I will not use the adulation of courtiers to pay you homage with this singular production. My purpose, Madame, is to speak frankly to you; I have not awaited the epoch of liberty to thus explain myself; I bestirred myself as energetically in a time when the blindness of despots punished such noble audacity.

When the whole empire accused you and held you responsible for its calamities, I alone in a time of trouble and storm, I alone had the strength to take up your defense. I could never convince myself that a princess, raised in the midst of grandeur, had all the vices of baseness.

Yes, Madame, when I saw the sword raised against you, I threw my observations between that sword and you, but today when I see who is observed near the crowd of useless hirelings, and [when I see] that she is restrained by fear of the laws, I will tell you, Madame, what I did not say then.

If the foreigner bears arms into France, you are no longer in my eyes this falsely accused Queen, this attractive Queen, but an implacable enemy of the French. Oh, Madame, bear in mind that you are mother and wife; employ all your credit for the return of the Princes. This credit, if wisely applied, strengthens the father's crown, saves it for the son, and reconciles you to the love of the French. This worthy negotiation is the true duty of a queen. Intrigue, cabals, bloody projects will precipitate your fall, if it is possible to suspect that you are capable of such plots.

Madame, may a nobler function characterize you, excite your ambition, and fix your attentions. Only one whom chance has elevated to an eminent position can assume the task of lending weight to the progress of the Rights of Woman and of hastening its success. If you were less well informed, Madame, I might fear that your individual interests would outweigh those of your sex. You love glory; think, Madame, the greatest crimes immortalize one as much as the greatest virtues, but what a different fame in the annals of history! The one is ceaselessly taken as an example, and the other is eternally the execration of the human race.

It will never be a crime for you to work for the restoration of customs, to give your sex all the firmness of which it is capable. This is not the work of one day, unfortunately for the new regime. This revolution will happen only when all women are aware of their deplorable fate, and of the rights they have lost in society. Madame, support such a beautiful cause; defend this unfortunate sex, and soon you will have half the realm on your side, and at least one-third of the other half.

Those, Madame, are the feats by which you should show and use your credit. Believe me, Madame, our life is a pretty small thing, especially for a Queen, when it is not embellished by people's affection and by the eternal delights of good deeds.

If it is true that the French arm all the powers against their own Fatherland, why? For frivolous prerogatives, for chimeras. Believe, Madame, if I judge by what I feel – the monarchical party will be destroyed by itself, it will abandon all tyrants, and all hearts will rally around the fatherland to defend it.

There are my principles, Madame. In speaking to you of my fatherland, I lose sight of the purpose of this dedication. Thus, any good citizen sacrifices his glory and his interests when he has none other than those of his country.

I am with the most profound respect, Madame,

Your most humble and most obedient servant,

de Gouges

The Rights of Woman

Man, are you capable of being just? It is a woman who poses the question; you will not deprive her of that right at least. Tell me, what gives you sovereign empire to oppress my sex? Your strength? Your talents? Observe the Creator in his wisdom; survey in all her grandeur that nature with whom you seem to want to be in harmony, and give me, if you dare, an example of this tyrannical empire. Go back to animals, consult the elements, study plants, finally glance at all the modifications of organic matter, and surrender to the evidence when I offer you the means; search, probe, and distinguish, if you can, the sexes in the administration of nature. Everywhere you will find them mingled; everywhere they cooperate in harmonious togetherness in this immortal masterpiece.

Man alone has raised his exceptional circumstances to a principle. Bizarre, blind, bloated with science and degenerated – in a century of enlightenment and wisdom – into the crassest ignorance, he wants to command as a despot a sex which is in full possession of its intellectual faculties; he pretends to enjoy the Revolution and to claim his rights to equality in order to say nothing more about it.

Declaration of the Rights of Woman and the Female Citizen

For the National Assembly to decree in its last sessions, or in those of the next legislature:

Preamble

Mothers, daughters, sisters [and] representatives of the nation demand to be constituted into a national assembly. Believing that ignorance, omission, or scorn for the rights of woman are the only causes of public misfortunes and of the corruption of governments, [the women] have resolved to set forth in a solemn declaration the natural, inalienable, and sacred rights of woman in order that this declaration, constantly exposed before all the members of the society, will ceaselessly remind them of their rights and duties; in order that the authoritative acts of women and the authoritative acts of men may be at any moment compared with and respectful of the purpose of all political institutions; and in order that citizens' demands, henceforth based on simple and incontestable principles, will always support the constitution, good morals, and the happiness of all.

Consequently, the sex that is as superior in beauty as it is in courage during the sufferings of maternity recognizes and declares in the presence and under the auspices of the Supreme Being, the following Rights of Woman and of Female Citizens.

Article I

Woman is born free and lives equal to man in her rights. Social distinctions can be based only on the common utility.

Article II

The purpose of any political association is the conservation of the natural and imprescriptible rights of woman and man; these rights are liberty, property, security, and especially resistance to oppression.

Article III

The principle of all sovereignty rests essentially with the nation, which is nothing but the union of woman and man; no body and no individual can exercise any authority which does not come expressly from it [the nation].

Article IV

Liberty and justice consist of restoring all that belongs to others; thus, the only limits on the exercise of the natural rights of woman are perpetual male tyranny; these limits are to be reformed by the laws of nature and reason.

Article V

Laws of nature and reason proscribe all acts harmful to society; everything which is not prohibited by these wise and divine laws cannot be prevented, and no one can be constrained to do what they do not command.

Article VI

The law must be the expression of the general will; all female and male citizens must contribute either personally or through their representatives to its formation; it must be the same for all: male and female citizens, being equal in the eyes of the law, must be equally admitted to all honors, positions, and public employment according to their capacity and without other distinctions besides those of their virtues and talents.

Article VII

No woman is an exception; she is accused, arrested and detained in cases determined by law. Women, like men, obey this rigorous law.

Article VIII

The law must establish only those penalties that are strictly and obviously necessary, and no one can be punished except by virtue of a law established and promulgated prior to the crime and legally applicable to women.

Article IX

Once any woman is declared guilty, complete rigor is [to be] exercised by the law.

Article X

No one is to be disquieted for his very basic opinions; woman has the right to mount the scaffold; she must equally have the right to mount the rostrum, provided that her demonstrations do not disturb the legally established public order.

Article XI

The free communication of thoughts and opinions is one of the most precious rights of women, since that liberty assures the recognition of children by their fathers. Any female citizen thus may say freely, I am the mother of a child which belongs to you, without being forced by a barbarous prejudice to hide the truth; [an exception may be made] to respond to the abuse of this liberty in cases determined by the law.

Article XII

The guarantee of the rights of woman and the female citizen implies a major benefit; this guarantee must be instituted for the advantage of all, and not for the particular benefit of those to whom it is entrusted.

Article XIII

For the support of the public force and the expenses of administration, the contributions of woman and man are equal; she shares all the duties [*corvées*] and all the painful tasks; therefore, she must have the same share in the distribution of positions, employment, offices, honors and jobs [*industrie*].

Article XIV

Female and male citizens have the right to verify, either by themselves or through their representatives, the necessity of the public contribution. This can only apply to women if they are granted an equal share, not only of wealth, but also of public administration, and in the determination of the proportion, the base, the collection, and the duration of the tax.

Article XV

The collectivity of women, joined for tax purposes to the aggregate of men, has the right to demand an accounting of his administration from any public agent.

Article XVI

No society has a constitution without the guarantee of rights and the separation of powers; the constitution is null if the majority of individuals comprising the nation have not cooperated in drafting it.

Article XVII

Property belongs to both sexes whether united or separate; for each it is an inviolable and sacred right; no one can be deprived of it, since it is the true patrimony of nature, unless the legally determined public need obviously dictates it, and then only with a just and prior indemnity.

Postscript

Woman, wake up; the tocsin of reason is being heard throughout the whole universe; discover your rights. The powerful empire of nature is no longer surrounded by prejudice, fanaticism, superstition, and lies. The flame of truth has dispersed all the clouds of folly and usurpation. Enslaved man has multiplied his strength and needs recourse to yours to break his chains. Having become free, he has become unjust to his companion. Oh, women, women! When will you cease to be blind? What advantage have you received from the Revolution? A more pronounced scorn, a more marked disdain. In the centuries of corruption you ruled only over the weakness of men. The reclamation of your patrimony, based on the wise decrees of nature – what have you to dread from such a fine undertaking? The *bon mot* of the legislator of the marriage of Cana? Do you fear that our French legislators, correctors of that morality, long ensnared by political practices now out of date, will only say again to you: women, what is there in common between you and us? Everything, you will have to answer. If they persist in their weakness in putting this non sequitur in contradiction to their principles, courageously oppose the force of reason to the empty pretentions of superiority; unite yourselves beneath the standards of philosophy; deploy all the energy of your character, and you will soon see these haughty men, not groveling at your feet as servile adorers, but proud to share with you the treasures of the Supreme Being. Regardless of what barriers confront you, it is in your power to free yourselves; you have only to want to. Let us pass now to the shocking tableau of what you have been in society; and since national education is in question at this moment, let us see whether our wise legislators will think judiciously about the education of women.

Women have done more harm than good. Constraint and dissimulation have been their lot. What force had robbed them of, ruse returned to them; they had recourse to all the resources of their charms, and the most irreproachable person did not resist them. Poison and the sword were both subject to them; they commanded in crime as in fortune. The French government, especially, depended throughout the centuries on the nocturnal administration of women; the cabinet kept no secret from their indiscretion; ambassadorial post, command, ministry, presidency, pontificate, college of cardinals; finally, anything which characterizes the folly of men, profane and sacred, all have been subject to the cupidity and ambition of this sex, formerly contemptible and respected, and since the revolution, respectable and scorned.

In this sort of contradictory situation, what remarks could I not make! I have but a moment to make them, but this moment will fix the attention of the remotest posterity. Under the Old Regime, all was vicious, all was guilty; but could not the amelioration of conditions be perceived even in the substance of vices? A woman only had to be beautiful or amiable; when she possessed these two advantages, she saw a hundred fortunes at her feet. If she did not profit from them, she had a bizarre character or a rare philosophy which made her scorn wealth; then she was deemed to be like a crazy woman; the most indecent made herself respected with gold; commerce in women was a kind of industry in the first class [of society], which, henceforth, will have no more credit. If it still had it, the revolution would be lost, and under the new relationships we would always be corrupted; however, reason can always be deceived [into believing] that any other road to fortune is closed to the woman whom a man buys, like the slave on the African coasts. The difference is great; that is known. The slave is commanded by the master; but if the master gives her liberty without recompense, and at an age when the slave has lost all her charms, what will become of this unfortunate woman? The victim of scorn, even the doors of charity are closed to her; she is poor and old, they say; why did she not know how to make her fortune? Reason finds other examples that are even more touching. A young, inexperienced woman, seduced by a man whom she loves, will abandon her parents to follow him; the ingrate will leave her after a few years, and the older she has become with him, the more inhuman is his inconstancy; if she has children, he will likewise abandon them. If he is rich, he will consider himself excused from sharing his fortune with his noble victims. If some involvement binds him to his duties, he will deny them, trusting that the laws will support him. If he is married, any other obligation loses its rights. Then what laws remain to extirpate vice all the way to its root? The law of dividing wealth and public administration between men and women. It can easily be seen that one who is born into a rich family gains very much from such equal sharing. But the one born into a poor family with merit and virtue – what is her lot? Poverty and opprobrium. If she does not precisely excel in music or painting, she cannot be admitted to any public function when she has all the capacity for it. I do not want to give only a sketch of things; I will go more deeply into this in the new edition of all my political writings, with notes, which I propose to give to the public in a few days.

I take up my text again on the subject of morals. Marriage is the tomb of trust and love. The married woman can with impunity give bastards to her husband, and also give them the wealth which does not belong to them. The woman who is unmarried has only one feeble right; ancient and inhuman laws refuse to her for her children the right to the name and the wealth of their father; no new laws have been made in this matter. If it is considered a paradox and an impossibility on my part to try to give my sex an honorable and just consistency, I leave it to men to attain glory for dealing with this matter; but while we wait, the way can be prepared through national education, the restoration of morals, and conjugal conventions.

Form for a Social Contract Between Man and Woman

We, _____ and _____, moved by our own will, unite ourselves for the duration of our lives, and for the duration of our mutual inclinations, under the following conditions: We intend and wish to make our wealth communal, meanwhile reserving to ourselves the right to divide it in favor of our children and of those toward whom we might have a particular inclination, mutually recognizing that our property belongs directly to our children, from whatever bed they come, and that all of them without distinction have the right to bear the name of the fathers and mothers who have acknowledged them, and we are charged to subscribe to the law which punishes the renunciation of one's own blood. We likewise obligate ourselves, in case of separation, to divide our wealth and to set aside in advance the portion the law indicates for our children, and in the event of a perfect union, the one who dies will divest himself of half his property in his children's favor, and if one dies childless, the survivor will inherit by right, unless the dying person has disposed of half the common property in favor of one whom he judged deserving.

That is approximately the formula for the marriage act I propose for execution. Upon reading this strange document, I see rising up against me the hypocrites, the prudes, the clergy, and the whole infernal sequence. But how it [my proposal] offers to the wise the moral means of achieving the perfection of a happy government! I am going to give in a few words the physical proof of it. The rich, childless Epicurean finds it very good to go to his poor neighbor to augment his family. When there is a law authorizing a poor man's wife to have a rich one adopt their children, the bonds of society will be strengthened and morals will be purer. This law will perhaps save the community's wealth and hold back the disorder which drives so many victims to the almshouses of shame, to a low station, and into degenerate human principles where nature has groaned for so long. May the detractors of wise philosophy then cease to cry out against primitive morals, or may they lose their point in the source of their citations.[1]

Moreover, I would like a law which would assist widows and young girls deceived by the false promises of a man to whom they were attached; I would like, I say, this law to force an inconstant man to hold to his obligations or at least [to pay] an indemnity equal to his wealth. Again, I would like this law to be rigorous against women, at least those who have the effrontery to have recourse to a law which they themselves had violated by their misconduct, if proof of that were given. At the same time, as I showed in *Le Bonheur primitif de l'homme*, in 1788, that prostitutes should be placed in designated quarters. It is not prostitutes who contribute the most to the depravity of morals, it is the women of society. In regenerating the latter, the former are changed. This link of fraternal union will first bring disorder, but in consequence it will produce at the end a perfect harmony.

I offer a foolproof way to elevate the soul of women; it is to join them to all the activities of man; if man persists in finding this way impractical, let him share his fortune with woman, not at his caprice, but by the wisdom of laws. Prejudice falls, morals are purified, and nature regains all her rights. Add to this the marriage of priests and the strengthening of the king on his throne, and the French government cannot fail.

It would be very necessary to say a few words on the troubles which are said to be caused by the decree in favor of colored men in our islands. There is where nature shudders with horror; there is where reason and humanity have still not touched callous souls; there, especially, is where division and discord stir up their inhabitants. It is not difficult to divine the instigators of these incendiary fermentations; they are even in the midst of the National Assembly; they ignite the fire in Europe which must inflame America. Colonists make a claim to reign as despots over the men whose fathers and brothers they are; and, disowning the rights of nature, they trace the source of [their rule] to the scantiest tint of their blood. These inhuman colonists say: our blood flows in their veins, but we will shed it all if necessary to glut our greed or our blind ambition. It is in these places nearest to nature where the father scorns the son; deaf to the cries of blood, they stifle all its attraction; what can be hoped from the resistance opposed to them. To constrain [blood] violently is to render it terrible; to leave [blood] still enchained is to direct all calamities towards America. A divine hand seems to spread liberty abroad throughout the realms of man; only the law has the right to curb this liberty if it degenerates into license, but it must be equal for all; liberty must hold the National Assembly to its decree dictated by prudence and justice. May it act the same way for the state of France and render her as attentive to new abuses as she was to the ancient ones which each day become more dreadful. My opinion would be to reconcile the executive and legislative power, for it seems to me that the one is everything and the other is nothing – whence comes, unfortunately perhaps, the loss of the French Empire. I think that these two powers, like man and woman, should be united but equal in force and virtue to make a good household. ...

[1] Abraham had some very legitimate children by Agar, the servant of his wife.

* See Olympe de Gouges, *Le Bonheur primitif de l'homme, ou les Rêveries patriotiques* (Amsterdam and Paris, 1789).

A9 Letter from Nicolas Rouault to his brother, Paris, 4 May 1792

From Nicolas Rouault (1976) *Gazette d'un Parisien sous la Revolution, Lettres à son frère, 1783–1796*, Paris, Librairie Académique Perresi, pp.284–5 (extract translated by Arthur Marwick).

I no longer pay attention, my dear brother, to what is said in the National Assembly, and in the Jacobin club. I am completely directionless; I am strongly inclined to renounce the interest I have taken so far in this great drama of the revolution and to think no more of it than if I were a thousand leagues away ...

What do you want me to tell you about the current turmoil in ideas and opinions? Everywhere people are shouting that the king is betraying us, that the generals are betraying us, that no one can be trusted; that the *Austrian Committee* is caught in flagrant misbehaviour; that in six weeks Paris will be taken by the Austrians, etc ... These are things to make one look closely at the patriots and the royalists. Read the speech given by deputy Isnard in the Assembly on the 15th; read the denunciation of the Austrian Committee delivered in the Assembly yesterday by Brissot and Gensonné, and you tell me what one ought to think about the royal situation and our own. People talk of dispatching to Orleans M. de Montmorin and several other persons attached to the king and queen, as well as the Minister of Justice, Duport du Tertre Grand Protector of the *Club of the Holy Chapel*, who is reproached with having furtively removed from the Committee of Surveillance papers of great significance to the court, including declarations and accusations ... I don't know if it was the Justice of the Peace Etienne la Rivière who helped him to do this, but that former elector of 89, the same one who took Barthier, the intendant, from Compiègne to Paris, has just been sent to Orleans where he kept company with a minister, Delessart.

Adieu, we are sitting on a volcano ready to burst into flames.

A10 Extracts from the decree regulating divorce, 20 September 1792

From John Hall Stewart (1951) *A Documentary Survey of the French Revolution*, New York, Macmillan, pp.333–4.

(i)   Marriage may be dissolved by divorce.

(ii) Divorce shall take place by mutual consent of husband and wife.

(iii) One of the parties may have divorce pronounced on the mere allegation of incompatibility of disposition or character.

A11 Extracts from the second propagandist decree, 15 December 1792

From John Hall Stewart (1951) *A Documentary Survey of the French Revolution*, New York, Macmillan, pp.382–3.

1 In territories which are or may be occupied by the armies of the Republic, the generals shall proclaim immediately, in the name of the French nation, the sovereignty of the people, the suppression of all established authorities and of existing imposts or taxes, the abolition of the tithe, of feudalism, of seigneurial rights, both feudal and *censual*, fixed or contingent, of *banalités*, of real and personal servitude, of hunting and fishing privileges, of *corvées*, of nobility, and generally of all privileges.

2 They shall announce to the people that they bring it peace, aid, fraternity, liberty, and equality ...

5 The provisional administration, elected by the people, shall be responsible for the surveillance and administration of matters placed under the safeguard and protection of the French Republic It may institute taxes, provided, however, that they are not borne by the indigent and hard-working portion of the population.

6 As soon as the provisional administration has been organized, the National Convention shall appoint commissioners from within its own body to go to fraternize with it ...

9 The provisional administration elected by the people, and the functions of the national commissioners shall terminate as soon as the inhabitants, after having declared the sovereignty and independence of the people, liberty and equality, have organized a form of free and popular government.

10 A statement shall be made of the expenses which the French Republic has incurred for the common defence, and of the sums which it may have received, and the French nation shall make arrangements with the established government for whatever is due; and, in case the common interest requires the troops of the Republic to remain upon foreign territory beyond that time, it shall take suitable measures to provide for their maintenance.

11 The French nation declares that it will treat as an enemy of the people anyone who, refusing liberty and equality, or renouncing them, might wish to preserve, recall, or treat with the prince and the privileged castes ...

A12 Extracts from the proclamation of the Convention concerning the events of 31 May and 1 June 1793 (promulgated 1 June 1793, published in official newspaper, *Moniteur*, on 3 June 1793)

From John Hall Stewart (1951) *A Documentary Survey of the French Revolution*, New York, Macmillan, pp.446–7.

Frenchmen, a great movement has arisen in Paris, the enemies of the Republic are going to hasten to present it to you as a great misfortune; they are going to tell you that the tocsin and the alarm cannon have kept this immense city in terror for a night and a day; that thousands of armed men, emerging confusedly from all sections, have hurled themselves around the National Convention, and have dictated to it their will as the law of the Republic. Frenchmen, your representatives are convinced that the happiness of empires can be founded only upon truth, and they are going to tell it to you ...

Liberty of opinions has again shown itself, even in the heat of the debates of the Convention. In asking the redress of their grievances with some exaggeration inseparable from civic zeal, but with that pride which characterizes free men, the petitioners swore to die for the maintenance of the law, for the unity and indivisibility of the Republic, and for the security of the national representation ...

Frenchmen, you do not doubt that on that occasion ambition, malevolence, and aristocracy were on the watch, always ready to take advantage of circumstances; you do not doubt that false patriots, subsidised by our enemies, were redoubling their efforts to achieve their ends by precipitating good citizens into dangerous excesses. But the vast majority of a people strongly in favour of equality, liberty, and property has once again foiled their hopes and frustrated their plans ...

Thus all the events benefit liberty. Let us together hasten the moment of consolidating it by a republican constitution. Your representatives have just taken a solemn oath to form, within a few days, that indissoluble bond of all the departments. They summon you to a fraternal reunion for that date of the 10th of August, which will always be the anniversary of the acquisition of liberty.

It is there that you will promise to abhor the monarchy which would subject you to domestic oppression, and the federalism which would deliver you powerless to foreign tyrants.

Citizens of Paris, you have seen that the confidence of the National Convention has never been alienated from you; you have seen that it takes pleasure in deliberating in the midst of a people in whom the love of liberty is a passion, and of a city which the efforts of an entire century have made the centre of sciences and the threshold of enlightenment, for Europe as well as for France.

A13 Extract from the decree establishing the *levée en masse*, 23 August 1793

From J.M. Thompson (1933) *French Revolution Documents, 1789–94,* Blackwell, pp.255–6.

(i) From this time, until the enemies of France have been expelled from the territory of the Republic, all Frenchmen are in a state of permanent requisition for the army. The young men will go to fight; married men will forge arms and transport food and supplies; women will make tents and uniforms and work in hospitals; children will find old rags for bandages; old men will appear in public places to excite the courage of warriors, the hatred of kings, and the unity of the Republic.

(ii) Public buildings will be converted into barracks, public squares into armament workshops, the soil of cellars will be washed to extract saltpetre.

(iii) Rifles will be confined exclusively to those who march to fight the enemy; military service in the interior will be performed with sporting guns and side-arms.

(iv) Riding horses will be requisitioned for the cavalry corps; draught horses, other than those used in agriculture, will pull artillery and stores.

(v) The Committee of Public Safety is charged with the taking of all measures to establish, without delay, an extraordinary factory for arms of all kinds, to cater for the determination and energy of the French people; it is consequently authorised to form as many establishments, factories, workshops and mills as are necessary to carry out the work, as well as requiring, for this purpose, throughout the Republic, craftsmen and workers who can contribute to its success; for this object there is a sum of 30 millions at the disposal of the ministry of war ...

(viii) The levée shall be general. Unmarried citizens or childless widowers, from eighteen to twenty-five years, shall go first; they shall meet without delay, at the chief town of their districts, where they shall practice manual exercise daily, while awaiting the hour of departure ...

(xi) The battalion organized in each district shall be united under a banner bearing the inscription: *The French people risen against tyrants.*

A14   Extracts from the law of 22 Prairial, 10 June 1794

From John Hall Stewart (1951) *A Documentary Survey of the French Revolution,* New York, Macmillan, pp.528–31.

4   The Revolutionary Tribunal is instituted to punish the enemies of the people.

5   The enemies of the people are those who seek to destroy public liberty, either by force or by cunning.

6   The following are deemed enemies of the people: those who have instigated the re-establishment of monarchy, or have sought to disparage or dissolve the National Convention and the revolutionary and republican government of which it is the centre ... [6 paras omitted]

Those who have sought to mislead opinion and to prevent the instruction of the people, to deprave morals and to corrupt the public conscience, to impair the energy and the purity of revolutionary and republican principles, or to impede the progress thereof, either by counter-revolutionary or insidious writings, or by any other machination ... [3 paras omitted]

7   The penalty provided for all offences under the jurisdiction of the Revolutionary Tribunal is death ...

9   Every citizen has the right to seize conspirators and counter-revolutionaries, and to arraign them before the magistrates. He is required to denounce them as soon as he knows of them ...

18   The public prosecutor may not, on his own authority, discharge an accused person sent to the Tribunal ... no accused person may be discharged from trial before the decision of the chamber has been communicated to the Committees of Public Safety and General Security, who shall examine it.

A15   Extracts from the proclamation of the Council of Five Hundred, 10 November 1799 (19 Brumaire, Year VIII)

From John Hall Stewart (1951) *A Documentary Survey of the French Revolution,* New York, Macmillan, p.766.

... With astonishment and admiration the peoples of Europe trembled at your glory, and secretly blessed the aim of your exploits; finally, your enemies asked for peace; everything, in a word, seemed to unite to assure you finally of the peaceful enjoyment of liberty and happiness ...

But seditious men ceaselessly attacked with audacity the weak parts of your constitution ... the constitutional regime was soon only a succession of revolutions ... From such a state of instability in the government there has resulted still greater instability in legislation; and the most sacred rights of social man have been exposed to all the caprices of fashions and events.

It is time to put an end to these disorders; it is time to give substantial guarantees to the liberty of citizens, to the sovereignty of the people, to the independence of the constitutional powers, and, finally, to the Republic, whose name has served only too often to sanction the violation of all principles. It is time that this great nation had a government worthy of it, a firm and wise government, which could give you a prompt and enduring peace, and enable you to enjoy real happiness.

Frenchmen, such are the views that have dictated the vigorous decisions of the Legislative Body.

In order to arrive more promptly at a definitive and complete reorganization of public institutions, a provisional government has been established. It is invested with power sufficient to have the land respected, to protect peaceful citizens, and to suppress all conspirators and malevolent persons.

A16 Extracts from the proclamation of the Consuls to the French people, 15 December 1799 (24 Frimaire, Year VIII)

From John Hall Stewart (1951) *A Documentary Survey of the French Revolution*, New York, Macmillan, p.780.

Frenchmen!

A Constitution is presented to you.

It terminates the uncertainties which the provisional government introduced with external relations, into the internal and military situation of the Republic.

It places in the institutions which it establishes first magistrates whose devotion has appeared necessary for its success.

The Constitution is founded on the true principles of representative government, on the sacred rights of property, equality, and liberty.

The powers which it institutes will be strong and stable, as they must be in order to guarantee the rights of citizens and the interests of the State.

Citizens, the Revolution is established upon the principles which began it: It is ended.

Secondary sources

A17   Mike Bartholomew and Antony Lentin, 'The veneration of the ancients'

From M. Bartholomew, D. Hall and A. Lentin (eds) (1992) *A206 The Enlightenment, Studies 1*, The Open University, pp.xi–xii.

Perhaps the most puzzling characteristic of the Enlightenment is its veneration for the Greeks and Romans. You will find Dr Johnson writing imitations of Roman verse; you will find Robert Adam promoting classical models as the ideal for the British grand country house; you will find Hume giving classical names to the disputants in his philosophical dialogues. A grounding in the classics formed part of the basic education of the elite in much of Europe, so that, as Johnson said, 'classical quotation is the *parole* of literary men all over the world' (Boswell, 1951, vol.ii, p.386). Why, though, did they not try to purge it from their culture, if they indeed intended to make a new world? Why should such a predominantly forward-looking movement habitually keep looking over its shoulder, back to classical Athens and (more especially) to Rome, as it strode ahead?

Classical themes provided a common frame of reference within which ideas and actions were projected. Both Frederick and Catherine defended their absolute rule in terms of reference to classical antiquity that would have made sense to their readers, whether they agreed or not with the monarchs' claims that their rule was really 'republican' in spirit. Furthermore, the vast and universally respected heritage from antiquity was usefully ambiguous. The most radical of eighteenth-century ideas could be, either decently or protectively, clothed in classical garb, and thereby at least given a hearing. Moreover, the pagan, civic, classical world appealed strongly to those who disliked the continuing grip of a Christian culture that was, in their eyes, a relic from the Dark Ages. This view is perfectly symbolized by Gibbon's recollection of the moment when he decided to write his *Decline and Fall of the Roman Empire*. It was, he recalled:

> at Rome on 15 October 1764, as I sat musing amidst the ruins of the Capitol while the bare-footed friars were singing vespers in the Temple of Jupiter, that the idea of writing the decline and fall of the city first started to my mind.
>
> *(Gibbon, 1891, p.151)*

The presence of ascetic, grubby-footed Christian monks, in the ruins of the heart of a once great civilization, offended his classical sensibilities. Gibbon's contrasting image illuminates the attraction, aesthetic and ideological, of the pagan world in the eighteenth century.

A18 Colin Cunningham, 'Reactions to Classical antiquity'

From M. Bartholomew, D. Hall and A. Lentin (eds) (1992) A206
The Enlightenment, Studies 1, pp.217–19.

'The only way for us to become great, even inimitable, is through imitation of the ancients.' This statement by the art historian and arbiter of taste Johann Joachim Winckelmann (1717–67) sums up a basic presupposition of much eighteenth-century culture. Whatever the reason for this attitude, it was, quite simply, so pervasive in eighteenth-century thought and manners as well as in the arts that it needs special consideration ...

The influence of the classics on western culture is continuous, and has a long history, although attention began to be closely focused on the pagan and classical world at the time of the Renaissance. Latin and Greek texts were translated and, with the advent of printing, widely circulated; Roman ruins provided exemplars for architects; Greek and Roman gems and sculptures began to be excavated and collected by the great families of Italy; and classical myths inspired painters, writers and musicians.

This new flowering of classical influence in the fifteenth, sixteenth and seventeenth centuries was a part of the inspiration of eighteenth-century classicism. Precise explanations of why that century was so mesmerized by the classics are impossible to find. We get, I think, some hint from the way in which English noblemen liked to think of themselves as living by the best standards of the ancients, and ruling as senators in their own republic. And the British system of government (in which a constitutional monarch, an aristocracy and an element of strictly limited democracy achieved a supposed harmony) was widely admired for similar reasons. Roman values, as described by Cicero, were praised; and the myths and stories of the classical world proved a rich and lasting source of inspiration in the arts.

The myths of the ancient world had long been a source of interest and were widely read, frequently depicted in the arts, and above all valued for the way they illustrated the human condition. With their many stories of heroism, faithfulness, divine protection and nemesis, the Greek and Roman myths and historical tales provided an alternative language of moral obligations and values to that offered by the traditions of Christianity ...

Classical influences in painting could take various forms, in the subject matter, the techniques adopted, in incidental details in the image or through allegorical or mythological associations of the theme. In portraiture direct classical references tended to be part of the background, as in Alan Ramsay's portrait of the 3rd Earl of Bute, or in costume, when the likeness was linked to an associative role that could be drawn from mythology. One reason for this was that practically no classical painting, other than on pottery or in the house decorations of Pompeii and Herculaneum, was known to survive in the eighteenth century. There were no painted portraits from the ancient world at all. Sculpture, however, was altogether different in that more and more actual sculptures from the antique world were being discovered, collections were being established and there was even a thriving trade in restorations and forgeries as well as the production of casts. These works of sculpture, besides being collected in their own right, were a source of influence in paintings and portraiture ...

The classical world, of course, was essentially pagan and so unrelated to the religious dimension of the eighteenth century, and it is important to remember that while the pagan classical tradition was very pervasive, this other Hebrew-Christian strand was also powerful. Equally if we pay too much attention to the Classics, we are in danger of ignoring the essential fascination of the thinkers of the Enlightenment with the world around them ...

The influence of the ancients, then, was pervasive, but not all-pervasive in the eighteenth century.

A19 Clive Emsley, 'France in the eighteenth century'

From M. Bartholomew, D. Hall and A. Lentin (eds) (1992) *A206 The Enlightenment, Studies 1*, pp.417–24.

The frontiers of eighteenth-century France were not greatly dissimilar to the frontiers of modern France, but it is worth remarking that parts of the north, east and south of the country (notably Artois, Alsace, Franche-Comté and Roussillon) were added during the reign of Louis XIV (1643–1715), while Lorraine was not finally incorporated into France until 1766. These additions were made in the same manner that the French monarchy had been building up its territories since the Middle Ages – by war, diplomacy, marriage. But the outcome was that there were many people living in eighteenth-century France who had little idea of exactly what 'France' was, and who did not speak French. More serious for the government and for the workings of the French economy, the way in which the territories of the monarchy had been created over the centuries had left a legacy of internal customs barriers as well as a mixture of local administrations and privileges which the monarchy occasionally bypassed or overruled, but which invariably reasserted themselves when the opportunity arose.

1.1 Government and administration

Louis XIV had ascended the throne in 1643 at the age of four. The early years of his reign, when the country was governed by his mother and, more important, Cardinal Mazarin, were marked by external war and internal disorder – twice the court was forced to flee from Paris. When Mazarin died in 1661 Louis declared that in future he would rule without a principal minister, and from then on, while he did appoint some competent ministers, he presided over the government of his realm himself and made the crucial decisions. He created a court of which the splendour became legendary even before it was established in a permanent setting at Versailles. Louis's court was a centre for the arts and learning; it became the model for other absolutist monarchs in Europe. It was also a centre where the most powerful noblemen, those who might pose a threat to the monarchy, could be kept under a watchful eye and showered with honours and offices to maintain their loyalty. Other lesser nobles flocked to the court seeking favours, office or patronage either within the court itself, or back in their own provinces.

While the monarch was the embodiment of all power, there was no means of ensuring his capability in the exercise of power. Louis XIV was competent, but his protracted and exhausting wars, and the privileges which he gave his nobles, were to have disastrous long-term results. When he died in 1715 the cracks were already beginning to appear in the edifice which he had constructed. Louis had survived his own sons and grandsons, and was succeeded by a great-grandson. Louis XV was five when he came to the throne in 1715; the Duke of Orleans acted as Regent until 1723, and for the next twenty years Louis was dominated in matters of state by his chief minister, and former tutor, Cardinal Fleury. Louis XV was not a great enthusiast for the business of state; he preferred hunting or his mistresses, notably the Marquise de Pompadour and later Madame du Barry. His costly and largely unsuccessful wars, together with the extravagance of his court, served only to encourage critics. His grandson, Louis XVI, who succeeded him in 1774, was well-meaning but of mediocre intelligence and ability. His participation in the American War of Independence had the short-term success of humbling the old enemy, Britain; but it finally bankrupted France and set in motion that chain of events which culminated in the Revolution of 1789.

The size and complexity of eighteenth-century France put the administration of the country beyond the capabilities of one man. Louis XIV may have made the decisions, but those decisions depended upon the information which his ministers put before him. Louis XV continued his great-grandfather's practice of ruling with councils of ministers. While a few ministers may have been guilty of misrepresentation, they did not all deliberately mislead their monarchs: however, they had to edit and filter the papers that were communicated to them, and sometimes these papers contained what men who wanted favours or higher office believed the king and his ministers wanted to hear, rather than what they needed to know.

Although France was nominally one country under an absolute monarch, one of the most crucial areas of the state – taxation – was 'farmed' out to

a group of wealthy financiers. While the *fermiers* (tax farmers) do not
appear to have been especially corrupt by the standards of the day, the
system gave the impression of corruption. Also, the exemption from
certain taxes enjoyed by the nobility and clergy gave the impression of
unfairness. Perhaps the taxation system would have been more tolerable
had it brought in sufficient money to pay for the court and for foreign
adventures, but it did not, and its critics cast envious eyes on the
successful fiscal system of England, often assuming that a strong currency
and solvent government were the product of a balanced constitutional
monarchy.

The variety of legal and customs divisions, and the different overlapping
administrative areas did not make for efficient government. Perhaps the
most obvious example of this complexity of overlapping areas is to be
found in the fact that the divisions of the country, called *généralités* and
directed by royal *intendants*, did not always share borders with the older
administrative *gouvernements* with their royal *gouverneurs*. In most
instances the *intendant* was able to make decisions and act on them but,
particularly in those provinces where there were old elected ruling
bodies, he might have to negotiate with these local 'estates'. The
provincial estates, where they survived, were dominated by the nobility.
So too were the *parlements*. There were twelve *parlements* until a
thirteenth was created, for Lorraine, in 1775. Despite the name, you
should not think of them as being like the British parliament. They were
law courts which had certain additional powers relating to censorship,
morals, religion, trade and industry. They also claimed the right to
endorse all royal decrees, and it was this claim which led them into
conflict with the monarchy during the eighteenth century.

The monarchy was aware that any rationalization of the complexities
within France would require the limitation, or even abolition, of many
privileges and that the people who enjoyed these privileges – the nobility
and the higher clergy – were not likely to give them up without a fight.
In the early 1770s, there was a serious confrontation between the
parlements and the monarchy during which the former were replaced.
However, on his accession Louis XVI restored them hoping, in this way,
to secure the support of the nobility for his government.

Monarchy, nobility and higher clergy in eighteenth-century France did
not share a common view of privilege and of royal absolutism; indeed
many of the *philosophes*, and some of the sharpest critics of French
absolutism, came from the nobility. Yet, in contrast to the rest of the
population of France, monarchy, nobility and higher clergy did appear as
a solid, if small, privileged block.

1.2   The three 'estates'

France had a larger population than any other European state in the
eighteenth century. There appear to have been some twenty-one million

people in France in 1700, and the numbers arose to about twenty-eight million by the beginning of the Revolution. Paris was the largest city in the country with between 600,000 and 650,000 inhabitants in 1789 making it roughly six times larger than each of its nearest rivals, Bordeaux, Lyon and Marseilles. But probably less than ten per cent of the French lived in urban areas; overwhelmingly, eighteenth-century Frenchmen and women were rural dwellers. Regardless of where or how they lived, however, the inhabitants were divided into three 'orders' or 'estates' – the clergy, the nobility, and 'the Third Estate'.

1.2.1   The first estate: the clergy

There were, perhaps, 130,000 clergy in eighteenth-century France. Over half of these were in regular orders, (the 'regular clergy') and two-thirds of these were women. The clergy were a privileged order being mostly exempt from direct taxation. They granted an annual subsidy, the *don gratuit*, to the monarch for this privilege. The Church as an institution was immensely wealthy with considerable lands and property. This wealth was controlled by the higher clergy, bishops, abbots and priors, who, generally speaking, were men, drawn from the ranks of the nobility. Some had, as well as wealth, considerable political power. There were also the secular clergy, that is those who were not in regular orders but who worked as *curés* (parish priests); there were also the *abbés* who did not take holy orders but belonged to the Church and were entitled to ecclesiastical benefits. The *curés*, though probably better off than the bulk of the peasantry, were not wealthy: they often shared the outlook and rustic speech of their rural parishioners.

The Catholic Church was far more dominant in the life of eighteenth-century France than the Anglican Church was in England. In 1685 Louis XIV revoked the Edict of Nantes, which had granted toleration to Protestants; this encouraged thousands to flee abroad; it also provoked the ferocious *Camisard* rebellion which continued for years in central Languedoc. The small number of Protestants who remained in France continued to be cruelly persecuted into the eighteenth century. The prosecutions brought against Jean Calas of Toulouse and the Sirven family of Castres, both in 1762, for allegedly murdering children who, it was asserted, wanted to become Catholics, were only the most notorious instances of this persecution. In fact, by the time these two cases were tried, the royal government had generally discarded its policies of overt persecution. It was unable, however, to carry many parish priests along with its policy of toleration. In the second half of the century several *curés* took action against Protestants in defiance of the orders of royal officials and even of their bishops.

Much of the Church's time was taken up with its social responsibilities within the state. Teaching in urban primary schools, in secondary schools and in the universities, was done largely by clergy. The rural schools, authorized by royal decree, were supposed to be lay, but even here the clergy generally had a say in the choice of teachers though they were not always able to get rid of men whom they considered undesirable once these were in their posts. The clergy also played a vital role in social welfare. By the middle of the eighteenth century all diocesan centres and all towns of at least 5,000 inhabitants had an *hôpital général.* These *hôpitaux* were run by nuns from orders like the Sisters of Charity or the Sisters of Providence. They varied greatly in size, and as the century progressed, their financial situation generally became more and more unstable. The result of this in Paris was that, increasingly, poor relief and supervision came to be taken over by the city's police. However, across the country as a whole, the Church and the *hôpitaux* continued to provide shelter for the many varieties of urban poor and indigent – for the old and infirm, for the insane, and for deserted or orphaned children. The rural *curé* generally supervised poor relief in his parish. Many *curés* put all their surplus income (i.e. after paying for their own maintenance, for a servant and for the minimal upkeep of their church buildings) at the disposal of the poor; many of them became highly critical of those who appeared able to help, but who refused to do so. Much of this criticism was directed against members of the upper clergy – bishops, abbots and priors who collected many of the tithes, leaving the *curé* with only a meagre emolument.

The first estate was by no means united in opposition to the development of the Enlightenment in France, although it was generally opposed to the *philosophes*, who were anti-clerical and held unorthodox views on religion. There was dissension, also, within the Church itself. The higher clergy were criticized by the lower, and there were some radical thinkers within the clergy. There were bitter and long-standing quarrels about Jansenists and Jesuits, which became mixed with political issues.

The Jansenists had been a subject of controversy since the seventeenth century, when the movement developed. Jansenism took its name from Cornelius Jansen, Bishop of Ypres. Its followers believed in salvation by grace, and denied freedom of will. Its doctrines were not unlike those of the Calvinists. Jesuit doctrines, on the other hand, asserted that man was a free agent who could resist grace, or else accept it, or achieve it by effort. The Jesuits, who were in a strong position at the French Court as advisers and confessors, and who had the ear of the Pope, succeeded in having the Jansenists branded as heretics in the 1650s. The differences later became political. The Jesuits and their supporters were Ultramontanists, accepting papal claims in France, while the Jansenists became associated with Gallicanism which asserted French independence from Rome. In 1713, a papal bull, *Unigenitus*, condemned errors in the writing of a Jansenist, Pasquier Quesnel. The *parlements* supported the Jansenists, partly from the motive of asserting their own independence. The Jansenist cause also won popular, patriotic support. Jansenism developed a mystical element too, which appealed particularly to the poor. Miraculous cures were alleged to take place at the cemetery of St Médard in Paris, at the tomb of a Jansenist deacon. *Philosophes*, especially Diderot, were particularly scathing about this form of superstition, as they saw it.

The quarrel between Jesuits and Jansenists flared up in the 1750s after the Archbishop of Paris had introduced the so called *billets de confession* (certificates of confession). Priests were instructed to refuse absolution to dying Jansenists unless they produced a signed statement that they accepted *Unigenitus*. The *parlements* supported the Jansenists by fining priests who obeyed the instructions and by beginning proceedings against the Archbishop himself. As the king supported the bishops, the matter became a conflict between king and *parlements*.

The Paris *parlement* took further action against the Jesuits in the 1760s. It investigated their finances, condemned books written by Jesuits, and closed their schools. These moves had much popular support. A Jesuit enterprise in Martinique failed. This failure, along with other financial disasters, was due to the Seven Years' War (1756–63), but Louis XV reluctantly agreed to make the Jesuits scapegoats and issued a royal decree suppressing their order in 1764.

There were, then, bitter dissensions within the Church, but questioning of fundamental beliefs was firmly opposed. Both Jansenist and Jesuit journals published strong criticism of works by *philosophes* and of the *Encyclopédie*. Stronger action still could be taken by the condemnation of works (as was done, for example, by the Sorbonne, the Faculty of Theology of the University of Paris). Such condemnation could result in imprisonment, exile or death for the offenders. In England and Scotland, people like Hume and Gibbon met with strong criticism from Church authorities, but in France, the Catholic Church, with its supporters at court (and in spite of its different factions), could present a really dangerous threat to the unorthodox.

1.2.2   The second estate: the nobility

There are widely differing estimates of the size of the nobility in France during the eighteenth century; taking an average between the estimates there appear to have been about 250,000 nobles in 1789. There were considerable differences of origin, wealth and ideology among them.

The *noblesse d'épée*, the nobility of the sword, were the descendants of the old feudal nobility to whom military service had been a way of life. As the administration of the state had grown more complex and less reliant upon the sword, a new administrative nobility had been created, the *noblesse de robe*. This consisted of men, generally drawn from the middle, non-noble ranks of society, who had purchased government offices which carried with them privileges of nobility. Initially, the proud Sword families had looked disparagingly on those of the Robe, but by the middle of the eighteenth century many Robe families had been ennobled for generations and were inter-marrying with the Sword.

Furthermore, Sword families were sending their sons into magisterial careers (traditionally the reserve of the Robe), while Robe families were finding places for their sons in the army. In 1781 the Baron de Gaix, scion of an old feudal family, could tell his three sons: 'You have to choose between the robe and [military] service ... The first of these two states is no less respectable than the second'.

While distinctions between Robe and Sword were becoming blurred, there could still be a sharp hostility between the two as late as the 1780s, and there was always a very marked division between the rich and poor noble. The poor nobility were to be found in the provinces. Their 'poverty' was, of course, relative. A few of those who pleaded poverty were on the fringe of court life, while others do appear to have been genuinely poor. There was a popular saying about the gentleman of Beauce 'who stays in bed while his breeches are mended'. Brittany had hundreds of these *hobereaux*, some of whom took positions as stewards, gamekeepers, wig-makers, even muleteers. They brought their produce to market in baskets slung on their right side, leaving their left for the symbol of their pride and their nobility – their sword. They plagued *intendants* and central government with requests for army commissions or Church appointments for their sons, or places in convents for their daughters. Their pride prevented most of them from seeking a way out of their poverty through commerce. They pointed to the *loi de dérogeance*, the law which forbade such activity; though in fact this law had never been generally applied. After 1750 the government was encouraging nobles to participate in trade and industry.

The wealthy nobility, particularly those who were to be found at Versailles or (as the eighteenth century wore on) in increasingly fashionable Paris, had no such qualms about participating in large-scale industrial or financial enterprise. Nor had they any worries about rubbing shoulders with non-nobles, particularly intellectuals who made their names with their pen by their erudition and wit. In the Parisian *salons*, nobles and non-nobles met and talked; in Baron d'Holbach's salons particularly, no subject was taboo. Discussing the nobility in Paris and Versailles during the eighteenth century, Professor John McManners concluded that 'the overall picture' did not reveal 'a caste ... graded by antiquity and lineage'. There was, he suggested, 'an upper class unified by money' which was, in turn, subdivided, and men boasted of or sought after their noble titles 'as admission tickets to lucrative employments or favours, or for their snob value, or simply as collector's pieces' (McManners, 1967, p.28). Even some of the nobles who mingled with the *philosophes* advocated reform within France; indeed, some of the most significant and most radical thinkers of eighteenth-century France came from the nobility. When the Revolution commenced there were liberal nobles ready to make common cause with different elements in the Third

Estate. But in general the nobility presented a barrier to reform in eighteenth-century France. The monarch could, and still did, create nobles; yet, at the same time he acquiesced in the nobles' demands that four quarterings of nobility be essential for most military commissions. The lucrative sinecures around the king were awarded only to nobles. The great offices of state became closed for the most part to all but nobles: of Louis XVI's thirty-six ministers, all but one were nobles; fourteen of his *intendants* were the sons of *intendants*, in some cases inheriting directly from their fathers.

There is a paradox in the behaviour of the nobility of eighteenth-century France. On the one hand they were creating barriers to reform by guarding their privileges and shutting off opportunities for non-nobles, but on the other hand they began to popularize terms like 'rights' and 'liberties', particularly the 'rights of the nation' and the 'rights guaranteed by Law' over which the monarch had no control. The *parlements* particularly argued in such terms. In 1776 the *Parlement* of Paris declared,

> The first rule of justice is to preserve for everyone what is due to him, a fundamental rule of natural right and of civil government, and one which consists not only in upholding rights of property but in safeguarding rights attached to the person and born of prerogatives of birth and estate.
>
> *(Palmer, 1959, p.451)*

Of course, the *parlements* were talking about the 'rights' existing in society in which nobles were privileged, and were using the terms to defend (or sometimes to advance) their privileges as nobles. They were playing with fire, for they looked for mass support from the Third Estate, and for a time enjoyed much support. But once the fabric of society had been weakened by aristocratic protest, members of the Third Estate could easily switch from supporting the rights of men as nobles to supporting the rights of men as men. The explosion of 1789 offered the opportunity.

1.2.3 The Third Estate

In pre-revolutionary France the Third Estate encompassed everyone who was not a member of the clergy or nobility: from the wealthiest bourgeois (who might own land and enjoy the seigneurial rights that went with that land) to the poorest, landless peasant – and many peasants were very poor. It has been estimated that about a third of the population of France in 1789 could be classified as poor or indigent.

The word 'bourgeois' immediately presents us with a problem of definition. The original meaning in France was simply 'townsman'. During the seventeenth and eighteenth centuries, however, it acquired a precise legal meaning and applied to non-nobles with sufficient wealth and leisure to live comfortably and who did not labour with their hands. Today, 'bourgeois' is used as a rather vague synonym for 'middle-class'; for our purposes, three points are important:

1   The legally defined bourgeois of eighteenth-century France was generally a person living off an income derived from property, sometimes land, which gave him seigneurial rights, though not noble rank; most 'bourgeois' employed domestic servants.

2   Although some members of the Third Estate made considerable profits from commerce, industry or financial speculation, so too did some nobles; and these pursuits were not exclusive to a legally defined bourgeois. Probably no one ever entered the bourgeoisie without being involved in trade, as this was the way to abandon manual work; but many also moved out of trade quickly to invest in land, in government stock, or in a venal office.

3   The holders of small administrative or judicial offices that did not carry noble status, and professional men, some of whom played significant roles in the ferment before the Revolution itself, were not necessarily legally defined bourgeois, though they would probably be encompassed by a broad, modern definition.

Below the bourgeois on the social scale of the Third Estate came the urban craftsman. Again, this was a broad category ranging from, for example, wealthy goldsmiths or tailors who worked primarily for the wealthy nobility, to modest shoemakers, tailors, masons, and so on. Master craftsmen employed the next level of urban worker, the journeyman. At the bottom of the social scale in the towns were the domestic servants (of the bourgeois or of master craftsmen), and then the day-labourers, men and women who had entered the towns either permanently, or on a seasonal migration from country to town looking for work.

Peasants were the largest single social group in eighteenth-century France, there were about nineteen million of them. But the word 'peasant' – *paysan* – covered an enormous range. Generally speaking, the peasant was free; Louis XVI abolished residual serfdom on his domains in 1779, condemning it as contrary to social justice. Only in a few central eastern areas did the peasant remain tied to the land. Peasants themselves owned about forty to fifty per cent of land. But land ownership did not mean freedom from the local *seigneur*, for the land was still part of his fief; if lands were sold, the *seigneur* could claim a proportion of the sale (*lods et ventes*); often he could tax certain basic commodities, and held the monopoly of indispensable economic instruments – mill, bakery, wine and oil presses. There were scores of similar 'rights' for the *seigneur* and burdens for the land-owning peasants. The peasant holdings varied greatly in size and were often fragmented; some peasants were landless, some were fairly well-off, though the genuinely independent owner-occupier was the exception rather than the rule. In France, it was the custom in many areas to divide an inheritance of property among all the children, rather than, as in England, passing it all to the first born. Consequently, the holdings often grew smaller with each generation. Peasants were therefore obliged to ensure their livelihood by tenant farming, share-cropping, labouring or doing domestic outwork (usually weaving or spinning) for urban entrepreneurs.

Bad harvests resulted in food shortages and these, as in Britain, often led to popular disorder and riots about rapid price rises. Sometimes in France this kind of disorder also saw the creation of bands of brigands. But while food riots and the outrages of the brigands were a headache for the local authorities and the police, they never presented a threat to the social structure of France. Rural France, in spite of the inequality of taxation and the burdensome last vestiges of feudalism, remained essentially stable and inward-looking: the peasants' first loyalties were to family and neighbourhood. Many rarely travelled more than a few miles from their native village in their whole lives.

As in the less rigid social divisions in England, women were kept in a subordinate position, indeed they were scarcely considered as members of the three estates in their own right. Some of the *philosophes* developed the orthodoxy by perceiving women as governed more by feeling than reason and as imaginative rather than analytical. When they contemplated improvements in the position of women it was largely in terms of re-evaluation of their domestic role by which they might contribute to improvements within society.

1.3   References

McManners, J. (1967) 'France' in A. Goodwin (ed.) *The European Nobility in the Eighteenth Century*, London, A & C Black.

Palmer, R.R. (1959) *The Age of the Democratic Revolution*, vol. 1, New Haven, Princeton University Press (vol. 2 was published in 1964).

A20 Olwen Hufton, 'Women in revolution, 1789–1796'

From D. Johnson (ed.) (1976) *French Society and the Revolution*, Cambridge University Press, pp.148–66, first published 1967, footnotes deleted.

The History of Women in the French Revolution has received at best limited attention. If Marie Antoinette, Madame Roland and Claire Lacombe have inevitably found their biographers and hagiographers, the ephemeral *clubs des femmes* their panegyrists and their critics, and the *tricoteuse* has been pushed into a respectable place in the most luxurious of pictorial histories, the attitudes of working women and their revolutionary experience remain an enigma, conceded but passing reference even in works concerned exclusively with the attitudes and activities of the working classes. Yet their rôle was both unique and important and their attitudes demanding of consideration. This short study is an attempt to begin to redress something of the balance by isolating a type of woman on whom information abounds, the working woman of the towns; the sort of woman the *sans culotte* most likely went home to, the sort of girl the married soldier at the front most probably left behind; the woman of the bread riots, of the revolutionary crowds, the 'mother heroine' figure of the *fêtes nationales*, carrying her banner with the proud device, *'J'ai donné un (deux, trois, quatre, cinq, six) citoyen(s) à la République'* (I have given a citizen to the Republic) and ultimately the worn-out, disillusioned, starving hag who sank to her knees in the Year III to demand pardon of an offended Christ.

To appreciate the nearness of women to the Revolution one must understand their rôle in the family economy, an appreciation crucial to our theme. One must start with the recognition that the family economy of the working classes, whether in town or country, was their natural economy: the family needed the work of each of its component members to support the whole. Hence, in a rural context, the man who had sufficient land to provide for the wants of his family had sufficient to employ that family. In the event of his not having enough, he or his family or both must seek an alternative source of income. In the case of the towns this was doubly true, for nowhere could the wage-earner, unless he practised some highly specialized craft, expect to earn more than he needed for his own personal maintenance, the rent of a shelter and possibly the upkeep of one child – a fact which the *Comité de Mendicité* spelt out in 1790 for all who cared to read its debates. Once this has been recognized, then the importance of the earning capacity, the labour and the sheer ingenuity of women and children becomes readily apparent. They were expected by their efforts to make a contribution and an important one to the family economy. Female labour can be easily categorized: for the unmarried, domestic service where payment was largely in the form of food and shelter but where a girl might raise enough to purchase the sheets and household linen which commonly constituted the dowry of the working girl; for the married, domestic industry in the form of spinning wool and cotton and the manufacture of lace. The last employed the largest numbers at least in Northern and Central France and in country as well as town. The value of lace lay almost entirely in the handiwork, for the quantity of linen or silk thread involved was slight and no expensive equipment was needed. Highly dependent upon the dictates of fashion, a luxury industry with an aristocratic and an international clientèle, it was on the eve of the Revolution, the most flourishing female industry in France even if the lacemaker only received a pittance for labours which would ultimately take her sight. In towns, women made up the bulk of the garment trades – seamstresses, milliners, corset-makers, embroiderers, ribbon-makers, glove-makers and so on – and lastly, in any community, poor women, the lowest cipher on the employment market, performed the heavy and distasteful tasks such as load carrying. Nothing was too menial. They carried soil, heavy vegetables to and from market, water, wood – anything. In the large cities, they found employment as rag sorters, cinder sifters, refuse collectors, assistants to masons and bricklayers – one can so easily multiply the examples. Where work could not support the family, then the mother had to have recourse to ingenuity. She taught her children how and where to beg or hired them out for a minor fee to other women who wanted to elicit pity at markets and fairs by the appearance of a large family or trailed her infants round from door to door with long and pathetic stories. She had a whole legacy of mendacity to bestow if nothing else: the children of Rodez, Richeprey, Necker's emissary in the Rouergue declared, are taught individual hard-luck stories by their mothers to impose on the passer-by to demonstrate a special claim to assistance. In the salt court of Laval alone, 2,000 women, mothers of families, were brought to trial annually for petty salt smuggling between Brittany, an area of free salt, and the Maine, against a mere 150 of the opposite sex. The importance of the mother within the family economy was immense; her death or incapacity could cause a family to cross the narrow but extremely meaningful barrier between poverty and destitution.

A contemporary feminist, Madame de Coicy, concerned to draw the attention of middle-class and aristocratic women to their subservient position in the household, emphasized the equality achieved within the working class home of the mother of the family because of her important participation in the family economy. Indeed one might, considering the importance of her rôle, go further than Madame de Coicy, and claim for her social supremacy within the limited context of the family. Restif in *La vie de mon père* has painted a patriarchal society but it is comfortable landowning society which is thus depicted. In its lower echelons society was far from being so. The strains involved in keeping a family together were immense. Poverty is an acid: it corrodes or dissolves human relationships. But it was easier for a father to opt out than for a mother to do so – easier for him to return home via the *cabaret* suitably anaesthetized with cheap alcohol to the squalor of home and hungry children and easier for him as well to clear off altogether, to turn temporary migration into permanent disappearance, or in the words of the Curé d'Athis, 'They lose heart: they weary of the strain of keeping a family on a wage barely adequate for one person and having done so they gather their few remaining garments into a bundle and hit the road, never to be seen again by their families'. The divorce lists of the Revolution confirm just this factor: in Metz, for example, 268 women sought divorce, with, for working women, separation as a result of the disappearance of their husbands in times of economic stress as the most usual cause. The results of the inquiry conducted by the bishops into the state of their dioceses in 1740 and 1770–4 are no less explicit: I am overwhelmed, wrote the *curé* of Bort, near Clermont, with women who come to me not only beseeching bread but accusing their husbands of threatening them that if they do not let the youngest children perish they will leave them and that alone they can manage but that even working all day they cannot feed their families; while a *curé* of Tours described a hierarchy of hunger in which he referred not merely to rich and poor. Women, he said, are not the first to die but they feel the pangs of hunger first because they deprive themselves to feed husband and children, and he made the inevitable and lengthy comparison with the pious pelican of the *adoro te* who gave her blood to feed her young. This is not to say that women did not drink, thieve, lie, prostitute themselves, indulge in every criminal practice one can think of, but that in general they clung more devotedly to their families and that this was widely recognized.

Indeed in time of dearth the importance of the mother within the family grew beyond measure. It was not merely that her deviousness, her relationship with baker, pawnbroker and priest became more important than before – there was no laicized parish rate as in Protestant countries and the poor had to depend on the voluntary alms of the faithful administered by the *curé* – nor just her assiduity in rooting out what food there was but that when all else failed it was she who had the right to spill over into riot, not the father of the family. By the end of the *ancient régime* this was tacitly not openly expressed: indeed one perhaps has to go back to Aquinas for the last discourse on the right of a starving mother to thieve bread for her young; but it certainly was, under certain circumstances, permitted to her to do so with impunity. She had to do it collectively and it evidently had to be a very abnormal year. The sort of women who were punished after a bread riot up to and including 1789 were those who in the course of rioting had destroyed property or shown themselves violent towards persons. It was this criterion which allowed administrators usually to pick out a handful for punishment – not that their share of the pickings were any greater. She also had to be doing it for her children, though it was rare to see a grandmother called before the courts either. I am not saying that men were never involved in bread riots – indeed during the Revolution they were markedly so – but that predominantly the bread riot was female, or rather maternal, terrain. One can make further generalizations about the women involved in these riots. In Bayeux, Troyes and Orléans those arrested in 1789 did not, with one exception, appear on the lists of those in those particular towns given an annual subvention by the *bureaux de charité*, so they were not paupers but women who in normal times could manage, proud women who were not counted among the destitute and who were fighting to remain so and to hold their families together. There is little doubt the most significant social division of the *ancien régime* was quite independent of order or class but lay between those who could make the proud claim, 'There is always bread in our house' and those who could not; and within those who could not, those who could claim there was adequate in normal times and those who had fallen below. That the latter were recruited from the former there could be little doubt and that most were recruited in times of dearth when prices rose and the family parted with what little property it had to buy bread and probably ran into debt seems equally axiomatic. The woman of the bread riots owed her intensity to her appreciation of the need to stay on the right side of the line between poverty and destitution. She lived constantly on her nerves but for her there was a worse state – it might be called living on her wits, on the caprice of voluntary charity.

It is with the type of woman who had to struggle to stay on the right side of the line that one is mainly concerned – though the destitute should not be forgotten: they comprised after all a fifth of the total population of France in 1790; but the destitute were not protesters, not rioters. The line between poverty and destitution was a psychological as well as a physical boundary, on the other side lay passive demoralization, the point at which the poor gave up and expected nothing.

The bread riots of the French Revolution then, whether the march to Versailles on 5–6 October 1789 or, to a less extent, the *journées* of Germinal and Prairial of Year III were *par excellence* women's days. Where bread was concerned this was their province: a bread riot without women is an inherent contradiction. How much they understood of the political implications is more open to speculation. Between October 1789 and Germinal Year III a lot happened to them however which was strongly to influence what ensued. It is their revolutionary experience in so far as it can be examined collectively that must now be outlined. Where did the Revolution impinge on the family economy of the poor: how did it alter the often delicate balance between poverty and destitution: and how far did these issues affect the attitude of women to Revolution?

In answering these questions it is difficult, given the research that remains to be done, not to be stranded between broad vapid generalizations on the one hand and a multiplicity of particularities on the other. One must at the same time distinguish between long term trends and sharp immediate results: not everything which seemed so blatantly obvious in 1795 had been so in 1790. No one had any conception then, and the question needs exploring much further, of the extent to which the economy of the poor was bound up with the abuses, institutions and society of the old régime. One does not know yet what happened to the 200,000 Breton families who had lived by salt smuggling when the *gabelle* was abolished. Cities such as Toulouse, Dijon, Rouen, Montpellier, Bayeux or Angers made cogent complaints of the disappearance in each case of hundreds of thousands of *livres* with the destruction of *parlements, états,* and the wealth of the church; money spent on consumer goods, as workmen's and servants' wages and as charity, and at least in one of these cases the laments were justified and it is clear that the economy of whole cities could be jeopardized if they were dependent upon *ancien régime* institutions. If a veil of ignorance as yet persists here, one can state more categorically the almost uniform drying up of luxury industries, many of them the preserve of women – partly due to the emigration of a wealthy clientèle, partly to the suspension of international trade and partly to the emergence of much more austere fashion. The lace industry, for example, depended on fichus, cravats, ruffles, petticoat edging, the paraphernalia of a girl on a swing in a *fête galante*. The economy of the working population of Le Puy, Chaise Dieu in the Massif, innumerable Norman towns and several in Flanders simply collapsed: hence the Norman and Velay lace riots of the Year II. Velvet, silk brocade, ribbons, embroideries – all these ceased to command a clientèle. In the classical gown alone is succinctly expressed the decline of at least five industries. Straight, austere, untrimmed by lace or ribbon, made of lawn, cambric or wool over a straight shift, it hid the waist and even put the stay maker out of business.

The second categorical statement that can be made is that ultimately when dearth and disease came in 1794 all the poor were to be affected by the total failure of French Revolutionary legislation on poor relief.

This legislation was to be the culmination of the enlightenment, the creation of a social utopia in which the poor were to be legislated away. Reduced to its simplest what was aimed at was: the assumption of the property of the *hospices* which catered for the old, the sick and the orphaned as *biens nationaux* and the direction and financing of them by the state; the total abolition of almsgiving, and *bureaux de charité* and the creation instead of work projects to employ the able-bodied poor at wage rates slightly below those current in the particular locality, that is work for the unemployed adult male; lastly, an annual subvention to the fathers of large families based on the numbers and age of the children. On paper it was at the time unparalleled in the history of philanthropy but those who drew it up neither had an idea of the numbers or kinds of people involved – they imagined a problem of unemployment, not a problem of the living wage; nor had they any conception of the value of the property of the *hospices* – they imagined it was huge and that just as the property of the church would allow the financing of the constitutional clergy, so the assumption of hospital property would go a good way to financing both the new *hospices* and the work projects. Two years were spent in compiling some sort of reliable figures but when this was realized, it became apparent that the issue was not mainly unemployment but the subvention of huge numbers of women and children, figures so immense that the *comité* saw that it did not have the means to cope. Even before the war came to reduce government finances to havoc, the government tacitly admitted failure in this respect. The net result was that the traditional methods of according relief were destroyed without any substitute. Moreover, in its need to raise money in 1795 the government assumed the property of the *hospices,* and the hospitals were made totally dependent upon the state just at the time when the war was demanding every penny the government could muster; many, especially in small towns, were simply obliged to close and that on the eve of the epidemics which chronic malnutrition inevitably brings in its wake. The frail safety valves of a society facing dearth were taken out.

Lastly, there was of course inflation and dearth which in some areas prevailed even with the maximum and certainly existed when it was withdrawn. Inflation and dearth which were to place a strain on the family economy of the poor in the traditional way and to demand that the women of the poor play their accustomed rôle but in circumstances which were markedly changed.

All these facets were glaringly apparent by the Year III but no one could have envisaged them in 1789. Indeed to do so is to pass from winter to winter without considering spring, summer and autumn. It is to imply that right from the beginning all looked bleak for all the poor: they did not necessarily, why should they, identify their fate with cleric and *émigré, parlement* and *états*. They did not necessarily see that they had any common interests with the indigent and destitute – quite the reverse. The hand that gave to some, under the *ancien régime*, or any régime, invariably took from someone else. The Trappist monastery of Bonnecombe near Flavin in the district of Rodez was in the habit of dispensing 300,000 *livres'* worth of bread annually to the destitute of the area but the grain used was drawn from the tithe paid in the main by the little landholders of the area. Now the destitute lost their bread and the little landholders retained a share of the crop which they much needed. The bishop of Mende usually accorded an annual 10,000 *livres* in bread to the destitute of the town but much of this came from tithe and seigneurial rights paid by the poor in the country. It all seemed and it all was incredibly complicated. It is not surprising that administrators of towns, districts and departments spoke half of the time in the future or conditional tense: when lists had been compiled, when estimates had been submitted and approved, if old régime officials would speedily turn over the information which they had at their disposal, if the government would accept a temporary or provisional estimate while a more accurate one was drawn up – then such and such a thing could be done. It was merely a question of waiting: the period was one of adjustment: Rome was not built in a day. In the meantime indirect taxes had gone for good; there were two good harvests and bourgeois ladies (as opposed to aristocratic ones who had done the same thing in the eighteenth century but under another name) formed *clubs des femmes* whose function was to collect voluntary alms (the government pretended not to notice) to help the destitute until new legislation was implemented. The *club des Amies de la Verité et de la bienfaisance* of Dijon formed in 1791 is utterly typical. The wives of department and district authorities and town officials met every Sunday; gave the populace an example of attending the mass of a constitutional priest and swore not to employ a servant or purchase from a shopkeeper or dressmaker who favoured a non-juror; and they ran lotteries to help families suffering from temporary dislocation and who might have cause to regret the old régime. One cannot as yet draw a clear picture of the working woman in 1790–1. In Bayeux, in Orléans, there are sporadic references in 1791 to women forcing *assignats* upon peasants at the market who reluctantly exchanged their produce for paper money, but the image is shadowy, unclear: she is a thing of bits and pieces.

In 1792 she emerges in anger at the interruption of supplies, particularly milk, which the country failed to deliver to the town, and increasingly her voice is heard as the protagonist of price fixation. From mid-1792 local attempts were made to stabilize prices and in Lyons and the large cities of the east, Besançon, Chalons, Vesoul, the impetus came from the local *club des femmes* whose recruitment expanded in the course of that year and changed rapidly in character from the rather precious early women's associations. Until they were forcibly closed by the Convention about a fortnight after the elimination of the Hébertistes, this was the common platform of the *clubs des femmes* and 'any other business' was confined to the war effort. Indeed it is with the war in the spring of 1792 that one really gets an indication that women had come to have an emotional investment in the Revolution and an intense one at that. Something of this investment is reflected in the tons of household linen – often the main assets of a working class family, the woman's dowry intended to last for life – which were sacrificed as bandages for the wounded. Chalons gathered together 20,000 pounds of sheets for this purpose; Bergerac in the Dordogne ran a close second and when the deputy of the area asked the Convention for a public expression of thanks he was told that instances of such patriotism were too common for special mention. Women of Pontarlier, a frontier town, contributed their wedding rings – the most pawnable piece of property any woman had – to clothe volunteers; in Besançon street walkers and women who had toiled all day turned up when they had put their children to bed to knit stockings for the soldiers at the front. In the summer of 1792 when war fever ran high, innumerable addresses were drawn up and sent to the Assembly wherein women stressed their patriotism and swore to feed their children the right sort of milk: the milk of 'bons principes, amour de la constitution, haine des tyrans' ('good principles, love of the constitution, hatred of tyrants'), or more specifically hatred of the Austrians, and the Piedmontese, milk of liberty and equality, or the uncompromising mixture on which the mothers of Clermont swore to nourish their young 'un lait incorruptible et que nous clarifons à cet effet avec l'esprit naturel et agréable de la liberté' ('a milk we shall purify with the natural, sweet spirit of liberty'). Moreover and much more significantly, they undertook personally to conduct the internal war while their husbands and sons went to the front: the war against traitors at home and not only actual traitors but potential ones, the children of traitors. On the outbreak of war against Austria the women of Lons le Saulnier, Mâcon and the Côte armed themselves with pitchforks and pans and declared they would defend their homes and children in the absence of their men, and if their men were defeated (the Legislative took exception to the implication) then they would make a last stand. The women of the district of Tarbes in the summer of 1792 armed themselves with kitchen knives and their children with ladles and set out to meet the Spanish. The women of Port en Bessin erected coastal defences lest the English should take them unawares. As early anticipated victory turned into early defeat, antipathy turned more and more against those suspected of internal conspiracy. There is little to equal in hatred and vindictiveness the venom poured out by women on fleeing priests and the relations of *émigrés*. September 1793 saw a spate of professions and declarations, a popular theme 'Comment peupler la terre avec d'autant de Marats' ('how to people the country with so many Marats') wherein women volunteered to breed little spies who would report on their playmates who were not being brought up on principles of *civisme* so that these unpatriotic mothers and children could be not corrected but *exterminated* and France's progeny could hence be purified. Old ladies called out in Lady-Macbeth-type language that children at the breast of a traitor should have their brains dashed out. When Pourvoyeur, a police official, spoke in the Year II of the bestialization of women and compared them to tigresses and vultures anxious for blood, the language seems rather strong but the evidence to support it is not lacking. Citoyenne Defarge, *tricoteuse*, the one stock image on which anyone can draw of women in Revolution, the hag knitting stockings for the war effort as the internal conspiracy is annihilated before her eyes, is a grim expression of the same thing and she is undoubtedly real. In every outward manifestation in 1793 women were more frenzied, more intense, doubly gullible, doubly credulous, doubly vindictive and the only exception to this is that they were less publicly garrulous than their men – but here it may merely be a question of lack of opportunity.

But how far was all this emotion a cover for the uneasy realization that circumstances were rapidly deteriorating? How far was she transferring her discontent, seeking some scapegoat, some acceptable explanation for the suspension of trade, the drying up of luxury industries, the very evident economic dislocation which was by now only too visible? Initially war can seem to unite a society in opposition to a common enemy and anticipated victory can too often seem the panacea to current economic problems. Both respects are deceptive: the last doubly so. The unity involved at a national level is a dissolvent at a personal level. War strikes at the family: it takes fathers and sons and what death does not destroy can be left to the effect of a long separation. This was certainly the hard lesson of the French Revolution. Moreover, the *sans culotte* was not too generous in sharing his new-found political importance: as the backbone of the local *sociétés populaires*, his evenings in the autumn of 1793 and the winter of 1794 were spent outside the home, in endless verbal demonstrations of patriotism and gratitude for liberty. The *sans culotte*, Chaumette said when he dissolved women's clubs in October 1793, had a right to expect from his wife the running of his home while he attended political meetings: hers was the care of the family: this was the full extent of her civic duties. Others have lingered on the pride of the *sans culotte* in his new-found importance in *société populaire*, section or as a professional revolutionary on commission, but in the meanwhile what was happening to his wife in isolation; how did she respond when he returned drunk on dubious alcohol and the vocabulary of liberty? Obviously the *sans culotte* in his home is a somewhat closed book, but at least one can know that the wife was steadily accumulating experience which was to sour her on the Revolution and all it stood for; that she was to turn against it sooner and with far greater intensity than her man, and in a way which was totally original, totally hers. In 1794 and even more so in 1795 she was to be confronted with the sort of crisis which was to try her particular rôle in society: with a famine which as usual was to hit her strikingly in her family and in her own health. It was to confront her with watching the unit she fought to maintain spilling over into the ranks of the destitute. While her husband was still talking she in some areas had joined the food queues and the minute she did that her loyalty was potentially suspect. For a time it might well intensify her hatred of the internal conspiracy: nourish her antipathy towards malevolent land-owners intent upon starving the people for their own gain by this artificial dearth and hence increase the violence of her disposition. But her nerves, her patience, her physical strength were already being stretched. At what point would she turn against the administration for its failure to cope? Some evidently were put more to the test than others. If the maximum in 1794 largely worked in Paris and ensured basic food at a reasonable price, the same could not be said for the little towns and villages of Normandy, for example, where the reluctance of the peasantry to turn over their food at a fixed price coupled with a deflection of resources to feed the troops in the Vendée and the great gaping mouth of Paris put women into food queues from February 1794 while the black market thrived. When real famine came with the failure of the harvest of Northern France and the great wheat belt later that year she had already been struggling for eight months to keep her family fed and that in a totally inadequate fashion. The death toll of 1795–6 was the result of *cumulative weakening* – not just the shortage of one year. The lifting of the maximum in December 1794 and the rocketing of prices only universalized a problem which in some areas was already advanced. By May 1794, seven months previously, the women of Masannay were already demanding the annihilation of people over sixty in order to increase the ration for the young. The first lace riots had already occurred in the Velay, and the women of Le Puy (if not the men who lived off them) were already identifying the cessation of the lace industry with the disappearance of the Church.

The woman had both to procure the food and to cook it; all her husband had to do was eat what she prepared and judge whether he was hungry or not. What she got was often the result of *hours* of waiting. She stood in the endless queues, each one a hotbed of discontent hoping that when her turn came something would be left and even then her troubles were not at an end. Often what she was confronted with was beyond her knowledge or resources to prepare. Rice was first introduced to Normandy at this time. Some did not have the fuel to boil it; others did not know that it required boiling and merely soaked it in water – what both tried to eat was a hard gritty substance in no way digestible. Then there were the queues for which the only reward was a ration of salt fish which had already begun to go off with the rising temperature of the summer months and which when boiled yielded a stench like ammonia. Just what of all this was a fit meal for a child? Even if the food ration consisted of vegetables, turnips or swedes, fears were not totally allayed for a pure vegetable diet was associated in the popular mind with the advent in children of summer diarrhoea which was a heavy killer of the young. And when malnutrition hardened into real starvation in 1795, when the government had abandoned price fixation and could be identified with the hardship, and when obviously the rich were still well fed, when the family's small saleable possessions had either been disposed of or dumped at the *mont de piété*, and when the riots of Germinal and Prairial had failed to bring relief, then the usual 'sexually selective' manifestations of dearth became apparent. It is perhaps unnecessary to recall the classical manifestations of famine: the death of the weakest, the young and the aged, the increases in the number of miscarriages and the number of still births – but one should bear in mind that the latter are the fate of women, that the whole female body is a grim metering device registering degrees of deprivation. A premature termination of pregnancy or infertility through malnutrition are the best things under these circumstances to be hoped for: better than knowing that one is carrying a dead child, motionless within one or that if one gives birth one will not have the milk to feed it. The mothers of Caen in 1795 were allaying the cries of their new born children with rags dipped in water – that way they did not take long to die. Then there was watching one's children grow too feeble to cry. The *silence* of the hungry household was something that struck St. Vincent de Paul in 1660 but it also moved observers in 1795. And in Rouen, in Bayeux, in Troyes the female death toll was far higher than the male – for the reasons suggested by the *curé* of Tours some twenty years previously. If death usually came to the adult from a minor disease playing on a weak body, the chances of confining that disease within the hospitals was non-existent. Even under the *ancien régime*, these were fairly frail institutions catering only for the poor urban sick but the nominal absorption of their property in the Year II by the government and the suspension of payments to them meant that except in the large cities where departmental authorities stalled on putting the property up for sale, the hospitals just closed: ceased to operate. Indeed, 1795–6 became legendary not only for the hardness of the times but for the total lack of any organs of public relief. The mayor of Toulouse in 1816 challenged a group of petitioners about the inadequacy of poor relief with the words:

do you prefer the charity of the *philosophes*? He needed to say no more: *la charité des philosophes* was no charity.

There can be no over-emphasizing that the revolts of Germinal and Prairial mark that frontier, that psychological watershed, that last weapon in the armoury – whichever metaphor one chooses to express the final woman's protest before watching herself and her family spill over into that silent twilight world of the weak and the worn out which is so difficult to fathom because so largely inarticulate: it was her last defence of her human relationships. One can perhaps discount the accompanying cries of *vive le roi*, or the Parisian one for the days of Robespierre, the rivers of blood and the time of cheap bread or the Bayeux one of 'quand le bon Dieu était là nous avions du pain' ('when God was there we had bread'), as more an expression of opposition to the present than hankering for the past; though one should take more seriously the women's cries for peace in Rouen and even more in the frontier towns of the East like Besançon and Vesoul where war fever had run so high in 1792. The cry for peace was one for normalcy: to call a halt – their great grandmothers had done the same in 1709 under exactly the same physical conditions.

The aftermath of Germinal had been indicated in terms of suicides, the daily occurrence of women and children fished out of the Seine, economically and emotionally bankrupt, but one might more profitably linger on another aspect: the revival of popular catholicism, perhaps one of the most striking characteristics of popular history in the last five years of the eighteenth century and one in which the rôle of women was decisive.

The intensity of religious fervour that emerged from 1792 was without parallel in the eighteenth century. Much remains to be explored of the quality of religious belief under the *ancien régime:* indications point to a general formal adherence to the faith without the existence of any marked degree of fervour and of areas where even formal adherence was diminishing – perhaps that most particularly in the cities which attracted the rural immigrant and where the pattern of religious worship was most easily eroded. Certainly anti-clericalism could always find popular support in the towns perhaps because here the wealth of the higher clerics was most conspicuously on view. Moreover the anti-clericalism which surrounded the implementation of the civil constitution of the clergy was an end in itself: it was not part of a wider movement, part of a programme for the achievement of religious purity. Latreille noted the falling off of observance in the towns from mid 1791 when clerics became involved with the pros and cons of oath-taking and the framework of religious worship became clouded. Without doubt, the equation of 'non-juror' with 'traitor', the result of the panic surrounding the outbreak of war, made the non-juring church the object of popular violence in which women undoubtedly played their part. The constitutional church never secured any widespread loyalty and a couple of years' absenteeism from worship was the background to the image breaking and desecration of places of worship in which women were often predominant during the Jacobin period. In short, the women of this study could feel they had actively participated in the disintegration of the Roman Catholic Church: they had done enough to feel guilty, and the existence of this guilt is crucial to an appreciation of why, in 1796, women ended up on their knees and from then on worked wholeheartedly for the restoration of formal religion within France, the Roman Catholic religion of the *ancien régime*, but endowed with a new vigour from below.

When Citoyenne Defarge, ex-*tricoteuse*, put down her needles and reached for a pair of rosary beads, an image to linger on if ever one was, she had to search out her priest and even force the opening of a church. From late 1795 onwards, even in cities which had demonstrated the most intense anti-clericalism, like Paris, this is exactly what women did. They brought back the formal worship of God. Nor can this be shrugged off superficially as both Aulard and Mathiez did in terms of women turning from the *fanatisme* of their particular clubs to the *fanatisme des prêtres*. This is only a half truth. They were not trying to revenge themselves on the Revolution. The cycle of dearth, disease, devotion is a common enough one: one has only to think what fruitful ground the hardship of 1816 would provide for the priests of the mission, but in 1795 there was something extra, contrition. The catholicism of 1795–onwards was the visceral kind: it owed its strength to the rigours of the times, the imminence of death from disease or undernourishment, disillusionment, shame, failure, the sense of contrition which sought as solace the *confiteor* and the *viaticum* and as such the sort of expiatory religion which defies rooting out. Women at Vidouville, in the Calvados, queued to have their tongues scraped free of the contamination of the masses of a constitutional priest and ensuing blasphemies; the wife of a fishmonger of St. Patrice, also in the Calvados, scrubbed out the parish church which her husband had bought for a song as national property to use as a fishmarket and which probably represented his one solid gain from the Revolution, and she and the women of the parish handed it back to a non-juror emerging from exile while her husband couched an impotent letter of protest to an equally impotent departmental authority. The women of Coutances fought with each other over whose babies should be baptized first and the priest in question resolved the problem by a personal estimate of which ones were likely to be dead before he reached the end of the queue; he misjudged in two cases but he sprinkled water notwithstanding on their little corpses. No government could hope to eradicate a church drawing on emotions which ran as deep as this: there was certainly nothing so fundamental in circulation in the last fifty years of the *ancien régime*. Such a movement had its vicious aspects. It was an essential accompaniment of the White Terror, as in the diocese of Le Puy where women sought out local Jacobin leaders, clawed them to death or perhaps ripped them limb from limb while the churches of that most clerical of cities were triumphantly reopened. But oftener the return to religion was quieter, less obtrusive, more symptomatic of the desire for a return to a way of life remembered.

Women perhaps turned to the church too for another fundamental reason: revolution, war, famine – these are the dissolvents of the family while the church stood at least for its integrity, its sanctity; the hallowing of birth, marriage, death; the cement of something much more intrinsic than the social system. When the cards were down and the scores chalked up, what really was the cumulative experience of the working woman from 1789–95? How else could she assess the Revolution except by examining her wrecked household; by reference to children aborted or born dead, by her own sterility, by the disappearance of her few sticks of furniture, by the crumbling of years of effort to hold the frail family economy together and what could her conclusion be except that the price paid for putative liberty had been far too high?

A21 Darline Gay Levy and Harriet B. Applewhite, 'Women of the popular classes in revolutionary Paris, 1789–1795'

From C.R. Berkin and C.M. Lovett (eds) (1980) *Women, War and Revolution*, New York, Holmes & Meier, pp.9–28, footnotes edited.

Colorful descriptions abound of common women in revolutionary Paris: market women marching with loaves of bread and bouquets to thank Sainte Geneviève for alleviating hunger in August and September, 1789; fishwives milling about the meeting hall of the National Assembly during the October Days, chastising its president, Joseph Mounier, for supporting M. le Veto; laundresses petitioning the Jacobin Club to demand the death penalty for hoarders and speculators in foodstuffs and bleach: red-pantalooned sword-wielding Républicaines-Revolutionnaires guarding escape routes and chasing Girondin deputies from the Convention in May 1793. All these and many others – cooks, actresses, lacemakers, charcoal-carriers – appear to be part of the supporting cast, adding color and drama, but not performing lead roles in the Revolution.

Common women did indeed have a significant impact on the men and institutions involved in revolutionary power struggles, and their participation was a departure from traditional forms of collective feminine activity and a step in the direction of participatory democratic politics. They were not feminists, and their goals were often the age-old concerns of wives and mothers for the survival of their families, but they learned to use revolutionary institutions and democratic tactics to secure political influence.

This essay questions certain assumptions about women's involvement in revolutionary politics that appear in recent historical writing. Some historians, especially those concerned with feminism, stress the failure of women's political efforts. Scott Lytle and Marguerite George in articles on the Society of Revolutionary Republican Women both state that the ultimate disbanding of the society was a defeat for feminism, and deemphasize the society's political influence during its half-year existence[1]. Two general surveys of women in revolution, by Jane Abray and Olwen Hufton, similarly emphasize the defeat of feminists and disasters for working women. Hufton goes furthest in underlining the political annihilation, physical hardship, and psychological guilt and devastation that Parisian women experienced after 1795. This emphasis on failure and defeat distracts the historian from investigating the network of political institutions that made possible a successful, though briefly tolerated, experiment in locally based democratic government, in which nonelite women were fully participating citizens.

This study draws upon documentary evidence which places women of the people in the political context of revolutionary Paris and shows the evolution in their political sophistication and influence that ultimately led to repression at the hands of Thermidorian officials fully cognizant of the implications of feminine political activities.

It is also concerned with clarifying disagreement among certain historians concerning the nature of political changes in the Revolution. The dramatic extent of revolutionary political mobilization in Paris has been well documented, but some historians of popular movements, notably George Rudé and Jeffrey Kaplow, have argued that the spring of 1789 marked a dramatic break with traditional popular manifestations in the Old Regime. The laboring poor, accustomed to riot recurrently but apolitically when hardships became intolerable, now acquired an understanding of the consequences of their actions for national politics; a political rhetoric from pamphlets, journals, and speechmakers; and, later on, a base for their efforts in popular societies and Section assemblies.

An alternative viewpoint places emphasis on the continuity of popular movements throughout the entire period of state-building and transition to preindustrial capitalism within a predominantly agrarian economy. These interpretations center on the problems of food supply, urban provisioning, and popular protest in times of high prices and shortages. The urban poor are not 'prepolitical', but motivated by a 'subsistence mentality', an ethic of 'moral economy', which stipulates that government officials – local, regional, national, and even the king – are obligated to intervene in the grain markets to police the people's food supply and protect their livelihood and security when shortages occur. Since women managed their family's meager income, shopped in the markets, and purchased bread, the dietary staple, they were often central figures in food riots and market disturbances.

The behaviour of eighteenth-century food rioters bears out the contention that they knew what they were about. The disciplined limits they often observed; their skill in frightening those who profited from the grain trade; their choices of targets for protest, whether bakers, grain merchants, customs houses, or the Parlement – all this evidence suggests political motivation, political awareness, and a certain modicum of political skill. The popular classes had no political power, except in their ability to threaten public order, but they understood how political power operated to affect their livelihoods.

Political change in eighteenth-century France affected political institutions in Paris and touched the lives of common women, foreshadowing the revolutionary experiences of their daughters and granddaughters. The administrative centralization of such governmental concerns as taxes, justice, police, public works, and natural resources that occurred during the long period between the seventeenth century and the Revolution had complicated and contradictory impacts on people's lives: their religious practices, their work, and their subsistence. A dramatic example concerned the cult of François de Pâris, which developed after 1727 when miraculous cures were alleged to have occurred at the tomb of Pâris, a saintly mystic whose charity had endeared him to his neighbors in the faubourg Saint-Marceau. The cult of convulsionaries was especially attractive to laundresses and other working women in the faubourg, who were allowed important roles in rituals and were considered the equals of male adherents. When a government order closed the tomb in 1732, women joined protests and denunciations of despotism. These confrontations led to a 'vague, but potentially important, political consciousness' among humble residents of the faubourg Saint-Marceau. A second example from the 1720s links women, government subsistence policy, and the Church. In the year 1725–26 the Paris police began organizing grain stocks to be stored (as sources of emergency supplies) in hospitals and religious institutions; in an account of January 1729, twenty-three regular female convents and seven secular female houses were listed as having stockpiles. The program created rumors of speculative hoarding and suspicion of government involvement in conspiracies to create artificial shortages and drive up prices; the linking of such fears to religious institutions was one root origin of revolutionary anticlericalism among the popular classes.

In the 1760s and 1770s, the government reform effort marked a radical departure from government's expected role as protector of livelihood. Turgot's suppression of the guilds in 1776 was greeted enthusiastically by some newly liberated workers, but violently protested by others, who demanded a reinstatement of controls on trade. There were many fewer exclusively female guilds than male guilds and only limited inclusion of widows in certain others, but those women who had guild protection feared its removal. The government's attempts to free the grain trade in the 1760s were seen as disastrous repudiations of government's traditional responsibility to provision the cities and feed the hungry. All these examples show that, whether resented as oppressor or demanded as protector, government was increasingly experienced by Parisians as a systematic and rationalized intervention in their lives.

On the eve of the Revolution, women of the people were subjects of a government whose officials at both the local and national level were trying sporadically to rationalize their fiscal, judicial, and provisioning operations. Sometimes women coped with these changes, sometimes they protested, and sometimes they rioted. They were not 'prepolitical'. They knew how to operate within the confines of their world: their parishes and churches, their priests and employers, their shops and guilds, and their marketplaces. But their power was ephemeral, The Revolution in Paris provided them with opportunities to evolve from subjects, sometimes passive, sometimes protesting, into participating citizens. On some occasions women made traditional subsistence demands for plentiful food at acceptable prices, but also adopted new tactics of democratic participation in a framework of revolutionary institutions along with extrainstitutional protest. Incidents of *taxation populaire* (setting the price of commodities by crowd intervention) might be combined with drafting and presenting petitions to the Commune, the national legislative assemblies, or the Jacobin Club. At other times, women combined subsistence demands with broader demands for public recognition of their rights as democratic citizens. Not only did women claim redress of individual grievances, but they also made occupational group claims and claims based on patriotic or republican interests. The principal agencies of these transformations in women's political roles were political journals, clubs, elected assemblies, and popular societies, all functioning to mobilize women for political activities.

What follows is a chronological examination of revolutionary events involving women, presented to document the thesis that the processes of nationalization of politics in a revolutionary setting generated and sustained a matrix in which women of the people evolved from subjects into participating citizens.

What was unique about the French experience in the age of democratic revolution was the dramatic mobilizing effect of events that began in 1788 with the decision to convoke the Estates-General for the first time since 1614. The procedure for electing deputies involved an extremely broad suffrage and, for men at least, the stirring experience of meeting together in electoral assemblies. Similarly, the process of drafting *cahiers de doléances* for the deputies to take to Versailles involved many Frenchmen in drawing up preliminary grievance lists. In the first year of the Revolution, other events drew ordinary people into the turmoil of national politics: the national circulation of revolutionary pamphlets, like the Abbé Siéyès's *Qu est-ce que le Tiers Etat?*; the proliferation of revolutionary journals after June 1789; the Réveillon riots in Paris in April and the subsequent fraternizing between royal troops and Parisians in the cafés and stalls of the Palais Royale; the resistance of some of the upper two orders to the demands of the Third Estate for the vote by head in the

Estates; the ultimate decision to create the National Assembly; the rumours in early July of a coup d'état by the king against the deputies; the conquest of the Bastille; the Great Fear in the countryside outside Paris; the decrees of August 4; and the food shortages and movements of people into Paris leading up to the women's march on October 5 to Versailles. The result of these complex and dramatic events was to mobilize Parisians for the national power struggle and to confront them with new or transformed institutions through which that struggle would be carried out.

In January 1789, as the hope of regeneration took hold of an entire nation, women identifying themselves as 'women of the Third Estate' published their petition to the king. They explained that they were excluded from 'national assemblies' by laws which they had no hope of reforming; they were not requesting extraordinary permission to send deputies to the Estates-General because they thought the electoral process could be manipulated. They accepted their roles as subjects, entrusting their king with the full responsibility of representing their interests and satisfying their needs. However, when they asked for royal guarantees that certain trades and positions would be reserved exclusively for them and that free public schools would be established offering practical and moral training to prepare them for honorable places in a transitional economy and society, these subjects of modest means, with trade-specific interests, revealed their awareness of needing new strategies and special government protection in order to cope with dignity and with a fair chance of success in a highly competitive marketplace.

In August and September 1789, following the popular insurrection which culminated with the fall of the Bastille and the reorganization of municipal government in Paris, the women of the people were participating in almost daily processions of thanksgiving to Sainte Geneviève, patron saint of Paris.

Jennifer Dunn Westfall has presented impressive evidence in an unpublished Mount Holyoke honors thesis that there were at least three discrete populations of these women marchers – fishwives from the individual market districts of the city; women representing trades, for example the city's laundresses; and women who came from a particular parish and who were accompanied by their parish clergymen.

These processions followed a prescribed route. Typically they took the women first to the église Sainte-Geneviève, where they offered bouquets and breads to the patron saint; one report noted that the women 'thanked Heaven for the conquest of liberty'; another report noted that they implored the saint 'to serve as the protectress in Heaven of our brothers who perished, sacrificing themselves for the fatherland'. From the église Sainte-Geneviève the marchers sometimes moved to Notre Dame Cathedral, and from there to the Hôtel de Ville, where they presented Lafayette, commander of the newly formed bourgeois National Guard, with loaves of bread and bouquets. Westfall cites one report of a young woman representing the female second-hand clothes dealers of the Halles and vendors from the Cimitière des Innocents as having lauded the Commander-General in these words: 'We have come to offer you the homage which you most like, that of our hearts. It is to your sublime virtue, to your profound wisdom that we owe our safety. We can only look upon you as an angel that was sent from Heaven to save his people. We are confident that you, as the common father of so large a family, will find a way to replace scarcity with abundance, arbitrary despotism with enlightened justice, troubles and disorders of which we have so long been the victims with calm and peace'.

What is so interesting about the processions is that these marchers, who expressed both their subsistence concerns and their new interest in 'justice' and 'liberty', were accompanied by contingents from the newly organized bourgeois National Guard. Apparently the women were not protesting, they were not petitioning – only participating in acts of thanksgiving. However, it is clear that at the same time they were making their organized physical presence felt in alliance with a militia which was under the direct authority of the new bourgeois municipal government, and which had been organized with the express purpose of defending bourgeois interests against the double menace of a repressive royal military force and uncontrollable urban crowds.

Some of the best evidence concerning the women's processions of August and September – and in an appendix to her study Westfall counts and categorizes thirty-four between August 18 and September 23 – comes from the diary of Siméon-Prosper Hardy, the Parisian bookseller. On Wednesday, August 22, Hardy observed:

> Towards the hour of noon, a kind of procession of girls and women is seen once again passing along the rue Saint-Jacques, [a procession] which one would say came from the quartier Saint-Eustache, accompanied by soldiers from the bourgeois militia and by musical instruments; these girls and these women returned from Sainte-Geneviève to drumbeat with two consecrated breads, five large brioches, bouquets, and two branches of vines decorated with bunches of grapes which they were going to offer to the Holy Virgin in the metropolitan church, having to go afterwards to the Hôtel de Ville. Several people were heard criticizing and censuring these multiplied and daily gatherings of *citoyennes*, who appeared, however, to have no object other than that of giving solemn thanksgiving to the supreme being for the visible protection he had just accorded to Parisians.

Three and a half weeks after this entry, Hardy's tone had changed markedly. Reporting on a celebration in the faubourg Saint-Antoine for the anniversary of the conquest of the Bastille – a celebration by members of the National Guard of Saint Antoine with young virgins of the district – Hardy noted: 'Many people found there was something terrifying in [the procession's] arrangement, composition, and immensity.

Sensible persons found these public acts, which could not be interrupted and of which piety was unfortunately not the entire motive, ridiculous. They thought that it would have been infinitely wiser for each citizen to thank the Almighty privately'.

Peaceful but highly organized and conspicuously escorted by the National Guard (which may have been reaching down to the women of the people for a popular base even as the women reached up and out to this bourgeois militia for support), these processions of thanksgiving, with the people's church and the new bourgeois municipal government as targets, can be read as dress rehearsals for the October Days.

The women who sounded the tocsin of alarm on October 5, 1789, and who gathered at the Hôtel de Ville demanding that Lafayette lead them to Versailles to get bread, came from some of the same market districts and faubourgs which had supplied marchers for the summer thanksgiving processions. When Lafayette hesitated, the crowds of women recruited sympathetic National Guardsmen and set off in the rain to march to Versailles.

What they did when they got to Versailles provides us with evidence that some among these thousands of women acquired a political education – in addition to assurances from Louis XVI that Paris would have bread and a king in residence.

Women who later insisted that they marched under coercion from armed furies nevertheless told the Châtelet Commission investigating the march how they had taken the initiative, how they had made their demands known to deputies and other authorities. Marie-Rose Barré, a laceworker, testified to the Châtelet Commission investigating the October Days that although pressured to go to Versailles, she ended up as one of the four women selected to have an audience with the king. Not only did her delegation ask the king for bread for Paris, but it made specific requests that he provide escorts for four transports to be sure that they would arrive there. The king provided them the escorts.

Madelaine Glain, a forty-two-year-old *faiseuse de ménage*, testified that she was 'forced, as many other women were, to follow the crowd that went to Versailles last Monday, October fifth.' But she also reported that she 'went with the other women to the hall of the National Assembly, where they entered, many strong. Some of these women having asked for the four-pound loaf at 8 sous, and for meat at the same price, she, the declarant, called for silence, and then she said that they were asking that they not be lacking bread, but not [that it be fixed] at the price these women were wanting to have it at'. Later, she returned with a National Guardsman and 'two other women to the Hôtel de Ville in Paris to bring back the decrees they were given at the National Assembly.' And finally, under escort of the National Guard, she was led to the district of l'Oratoire to 'convey this good news'. So this 'involuntary participant' in the October Days also turned out to be a woman who, having forced her way into the National Assembly meeting at Versailles, communicated the marchers' objectives to the deputies, and was part of a delegation which conveyed back to the bourgeois government in Paris the news that the marchers' demands had been met, and more.

In one account of the October Days, a journalist noted that women occupying the meeting place of assembly voted with the deputies on motions and amendments relating to legislation on the circulation and distribution of grains, and 'exercised ... the function of the legislative power and the executive power.' This essay has suggested that the summer processions in Paris can be looked upon retrospectively as dress rehearsals for the march to Versailles; but the playacting at Versailles shows that women were fulfilling an impressive number of roles for which there had been, apparently, no rehearsal. There had long been a French tradition of festivals when common folk put on the clothing and played the roles of mayors, judges, and other town authorities. In October 1789, the women comprehended that the deputies at Versailles were their representatives, not their rulers, and that they could playact at being their own representatives. They were holding a dress rehearsal for their performance as the sovereign people.

The thousands of women who marched to Versailles on October 5 were only loosely organized; but their alliance with the National Guard and their impressive numbers gave them the leverage that contributed so heavily to their success: they conquered in their demands for bread; and they conquered a king for Paris. The thousands of women who returned in triumph to Paris on October 6 had become part of a complicated political struggle for control of the Revolution. When they played legislators for a night, served as representatives to the king, formed part of delegations to the City Hall, and served as emissaries to their Sections, these women were learning through experience how their traditional roles in insurrectionary movements could be combined with new roles as citizen-participants to yield impressive results – to begin with, the satisfaction of immediately pressing demands for protection, security, and subsistence.

On the Champ de Mars in Paris in July 1791, two years after the events of the October Days, women of the people are again prominent among the crowds gathered there to sign a petition calling for a referendum on the future of the king's executive role. During the years 1789–1791, small numbers of common women had been admitted to popular societies; they were spectators in the galleries of radical clubs which espoused openly republican ideas.

In the winter and spring of 1791, members of the Cordeliers Club in Paris used correspondence, delegations, and petitions linking the growing number of popular societies founded to instruct the people and oversee the conduct of officials. In May, representatives from the Cordeliers and fraternal societies formed a central committee led by François Robert to protest against the restrictive suffrage laws for election to the national legislature and to support strikes of carpenters, typographers, and iron merchants.

In late June 1791, as the Constitution was being completed, Louis XVI, who had resisted some of the National Assembly's earlier legislation, fled Paris with the royal family; he returned escorted by civilian and military revolutionaries unable to renounce a monarch who was at the center of the new constitutional arrangement. Now, republican voices among club members became stronger; political clubs, led by the Cordeliers Club, carried their call for a national referendum on the issues of monarchical executive authority into the fraternal societies. In this way, significant numbers of common men and women were alerted to the urgency and centrality of an issue – the legitimacy of monarchical executive authority – that was not directly related to traditional bread-and-butter issues that typically brought people into the streets.

A call went out from the radical clubs for a rally at the Champ de Mars to sign a petition calling for the popular referendum. Women were deputized by fraternal societies; they took part in the Cordeliers Club debates, and in debates in other clubs.

On July 14, 1791, women were prominent among members of the Cordeliers Club and the popular societies who gathered on the Champ de la Fédération and signed and delivered a petition to the National Assembly. Forty-one women, 'women, sisters, and Roman women', signed that petition – the petition 'of the hundred'. It read in part: 'The citizens present here come therefore with this [character] which they hold from the Romans; with this character of liberty which they will preserve until they die; to ask of the Nation's representatives that they not legislate anything definitive concerning the fate of Louis XVI until the desires of the commoners [les communes] of France have been expressed and until the voice of the mass of the people has been heard'.

Another participant in the petition signing, a young shopwoman and member of a fraternal society, was designated and deputized by her society to present the petition to the National Assembly. While engaged in this mission, the shopkeeper was menaced by the mayor and a member of the bourgeois National Guard, whom she accused of threatening to kidnap her and close and raze her shop. The following day, when she joined another deputation 'of thousands' which presented a petition to the Jacobin Club requesting that its members sign the Champ de Mars petition individually, this woman was in a position to ask that the president of the Jacobin Club protect her from menaces coming from the highest echelons of the revolutionary establishment. She had learned to identify personal and political enemies and the institutions that could be expected to guard her against abuses of power. She might well have been following a pattern of patron-client relationships – between servant and employer, or parishioner and *curé* – that was customary in the Old Regime, but she understood that the Revolution had transformed her source of aid into a public and impersonal institution.

When crowds numbering in the tens of thousands gathered on the Champ de Mars on July 17 to sign the final petition demanding the referendum, Lafayette called out the National Guard to disperse them. The petitioners tarried and the Guard opened fire, killing about fifty persons. Following the *journée* of the Champ de Mars, members of the Cordeliers Club were arrested or forced to flee; women were arrested as well; among them were not only leading feminists, including Etta Palm d'Aelders, but also the wife of a butcher who was active in Section politics, the wife of a wine merchant, and the owner of Hébert's print works.

Among those who marked the petition were women unable to sign their names. An eleven-year-old boy who testified at an inquiry into the Champ de Mars incidents noted 'that we saw many people go up to sign, among them, with her children, [was] an old woman, who, not knowing how to write, had one of her children sign for her.'

Louise Evrard, a cook, was arrested on July 17 because she insulted the wife of a National Guardsman who had participated in the events at the Champ de Mars that day. George Rudé has paraphrased her cross-examination by the police commissioner of the Section Fontaine de Grenelle. That cross-examination reveals that Evrard, who was present at the Champ de Mars '[to] sign a petition "comme tous les bons patriotes",' as she puts it, also knew very well what the issues were. 'She understood its aim was "à faire organiser autrement le pouvoir exécutif"'. She acknowledged that she was frequently at the Palais Royale and at the Tuileries – centers for the communication of political news; that she had attended Cordeliers Club meetings, although she was not a member. She acknowledged that her expression of grief at the death of the radical journalist Loustalot had found its way into the *Révolutions de Paris*; and finally, she stated that she read Marat's journal, along with Audouin's and Desmoulins', and frequently the *Orateur du peuple* as well.

By the summer of 1791, then, women of the people in Paris had begun to institutionalize their political activities within clubs and popular societies. There, and especially in the wake of the king's flight to Varennes, they became sensitized to issues of royal legitimacy and the extent of suffrage at a critical moment in revolutionary history. In fact, the participation of radicalized women in petition signing at the Champ de Mars indicates that they were looking critically not only at royal authority but also at the Constituent Assembly, which had failed to withdraw support of the monarch. Women who gathered at the Champ de Mars were willing to take a stand on revolutionary political issues that were not bread-and-butter issues. The extent of their participation may never be known – much of the critical evidence burned in the great fire of 1871 – but the fact of it cannot be ignored: in the summer of 1791, women of the people combined petition signing with club attendance, the study of newspapers, the formation of delegations and deputations – a whole panoply of political role-playing within revolutionary institutions that signals to us the expansion of their awareness of the potency of their political influence. Finally, the *journée* of the Champ de Mars may have alerted the people of Paris – artisans, shopkeepers, men and women of the laboring poor – to the serious and tragic implications of the split between their needs and interests and the goals of the revolutionary leadership.

Nonetheless, once the Constitution was completed (September 1791) it was generally accepted, notwithstanding the tragic incident at the Champ de Mars. The legitimacy crisis which that incident illuminated and exacerbated was reactivated in 1792–1793. Under the impact of critical events during the period January 1792–February 1793 – the overthrow of monarchy; new and intensified economic hardship; the creation or strengthening of Section assemblies and societies and new clubs dominated and led by *sans-culottes*; and the formation of a new national legislature, the National Convention – the common women, the *femmes sans-culottes*, stepped up the pace of their political activity and focused it principally on subsistence concerns.

The events of the *journées* of February 1792 and February-March 1793 illustrate the rich, complex combinations of legal and marginally legal politics of the *femmes sans-culottes* and allow us to measure their progress as citizen-participants.

The Sugar Crisis of January-February 1792 occurred as civil war raged between royalists and patriots in the French West Indies. Capitalizing on the crisis, speculators hoarded their stores of colonial products, especially coffee and sugar, in expectation of soaring prices. Working-class women, for whom sugar had become a necessity – they used it with coffee in the mornings and at lunchtime, as an energizer – protested the price hikes in petitions to the Commune and the Legislative Assembly; finally, when the Assembly failed to act on their complaints, they resorted to a traditional form of crowd violence, *taxation populaire*, in the capital's faubourgs and central markets.

In February of the following year, with a republic proclaimed, the *sans-culottes* were in a position to articulate, from their strengthened organizations in the Sections, the common people's demands: political and economic terror against the people's enemies and laws against hoarders. In a period of exacerbated subsistence crisis, *femmes sans-culottes* once again organized. They sent deputations to the Jacobin Society, to the Paris Commune, and to the National Convention to demand fixed grain prices and severe punishment for the nation's domestic and foreign enemies. On February 24, 1793, at the Commune, the revolutionary municipal government, 'a large deputation of *citoyennes*' asked for authorization to go before the Convention to demand that prices on subsistence commodities be reduced, and to denounce hoarders. Commune officials informed them that the Commune's authorization was not necessary; but they also urged the women to return home, and assured them that Commune authorities were preparing an address to the Convention demanding a strict law against hoarders.

On February 22, 1793, at the Jacobin Society, 'a deputation of *citoyennes* from the Section des Quatre-Nations' requested the use of the Jacobin meeting hall to discuss the hoarding problem. Robespierre the Younger objected 'that repeated discussions about foodstuffs would alarm the Republic'; the president declared that 'the Jacobins no longer were free to dispose of their meeting room during the day; and were absolutely unable to offer it for use'; Dubois-Crancé declared that the revolutionaries had priorities: 'first liberty must be conquered, that afterwards foodstuffs would be cheap'; another member voiced his fear 'that if the *citoyennes* were allowed to use the meeting room, 30,000 women might foment disorder in Paris'; Jeanbon Saint-André added that the solution 'would be to exclude from the popular societies any person who instigated discussion on this subject with the intention of breaking the peace'.

On February 24, 1793, several delegations of *citoyennes* appeared at the National Convention. The petition of a deputation of *citoyenne* laundresses read as follows:

> Legislators, the laundresses of Paris have come into this sacred sanctuary of the laws and justice to set forth their concerns. Not only are all essential foodstuffs being sold at excessive prices: but also the price of the raw materials used in bleaching have gotten so high that soon the least fortunate class of people will be unable to have white underwear which it cannot do without. It isn't that the materials are lacking; they are abundant; it's hoarding and speculation which drive up the price. You have made the blade of the laws bear down on the heads of these public bloodsuckers. We ask the death penalty for hoarders and speculators.

The president of the Convention responded to this demand with the observation that nothing drove prices up more certainly than cries of hoarding.

Another deputation of *citoyennes* from a 'fraternal society meeting in the locale of the former Jacobins' (probably the nexus of the future Society for Revolutionary Republican Women) expressed its concern that the price of subsistence goods be forced down and asked for the report on 'the law which makes silver negotiable.' A deputy, backed by the president, informed this deputation that the committees of the Convention were working on the problem and would report the following day.

A day later, having met with delaying tactics at the Convention, women took the matter of their subsistence into their own hands. The journalist

Prud'homme reported on the crisis in his *Révolutions de Paris* for February 25. Noting that hoarding, lack of bread, and high soap prices had evoked complaints and protests from the *citoyennes* of Paris, Prud'homme observed:

> Already bitter complaints were being heard in the spectator galleries of the General Council of the Commune. It [the Council] replied: 'Go take your complaints to the bar of the Convention'. The advice was heeded. Sunday, among the petitioners, several cried out: 'Bread and soap!' These cries were supported outside the hall by large and very agitated groups. The Convention took all that in with considerable coolness and adjourned until Tuesday, when the matter was to be taken up. Far from calming and satisfying [them], this resolution embittered them still more, and upon leaving the bar [of the Convention] the women in the corridors said aloud, to whomever was willing to listen: 'We are adjourned until Tuesday; but as for us, we adjourn ourselves until Monday. When our children ask us for milk, we don't adjourn them until the day after tomorrow.'

Police reports on the *journées* of February 1793 describe the women's alternative to adjournment, insurrection: their instigation, leadership, and support of numerous expeditions of *taxation populaire*, raids on warehouses, bakeries, and groceries, and sales at an enforced 'just price.'

The commissaire who filed his report on damages at the warehouse of Citizen Command on February 25, 1793 noted that women dominated the crowds; Command attested that 'a considerable number of men and a larger number of women appeared at the door of his house.' Command also testified that the women were there to remove soap, and then sugar, once they understood that Command had no soap in stock:

> First, several of these women asked him whether he had any soap, to which he replied, no. Seeing that a portion of them were taking a stand against him personally, he went back in. Neighbors and other good citizens approached these women. They assured them that there wasn't any soap, and in fact, he hadn't had any at his place for a year. One of these women, letting it be seen that she was pregnant by slapping her stomach, said, 'I need sugar for my little one.' Immediately, all the women said, 'We must have sugar.'

Furthermore, the commissaire's report shows that the women were not embarked on pillages; they had organized and were executing an expedition of *taxation populaire*: 'Then all the women streamed into the warehouse, and seized the sugar, brown sugar, and coffee that was stored there. Several insisted on paying, as follows: 20 sous a livre for sugar; 10 sous a livre for brown sugar; and 20 sous a livre for coffee.' Finally, the commissaire's report provides evidence of the magnitude of these operations: Citizen Command's total losses, as he calculated them, were 25,458 livres, 11 sous.

The commissaire's report on the events of February 24, 25, and 26 in the Section de l'Arsenal provides other examples of women's *taxation populaire*. Describing his midafternoon tour of a grocery on the quai des

Armes, where men and women forced him to accompany them on an inspection of the grocer's house and then returned to his shop, where they mounted an operation of *taxation populaire*, the commissaire noted:

> And finally, there was a woman, of fairly good appearance, unknown to me, but whom we would recognize perfectly. She was about five feet one inch tall, thirty years old, with blond hair, white skin, and slightly red eyes. She wore her hair in a demi-bonnet to which a rose-colored ribbon was attached. She was dressed in a *déshabillé* made out of linen, with a blue background and a standard design on it. She wore a mantlet of black taffeta and a gold watch on a steel chain. ... This woman did everything in her power to add to the sedition. She had gone on the inspection. And once they returned, it was she who set the price for soap at 12 sous per livre; and for sugar at 18. After which, the aforementioned merchandise on hand at the aforementioned Rousseau's place was handed over with an unbelievable impetuosity. Everyone wanted to pay, to be waited on, and to get out, all at the same time. We were compelled to take in the cash in order to prevent a total loss. The aforementioned woman took the aforementioned goods, for which she paid us, and we barely had the time to take in the money, hand over the goods, and put the money in the drawer.

Later in the afternoon, the commissaire returned to the quai des Armes, in response to reports of new disturbances:

> We saw a *citoyenne* there, well dressed, who was influencing people, and stirring up trouble. Having listened to her during a period allowed for this moment, we apprehended her calling upon constituted armed force for support. *Another perilous moment*, given that the people were opposed to her being taken away. Finally, we brought her before the Committee where we drew up a *procès-verbal*, and we sent this *citoyenne* to the commissaire of police of the Section de la Maison Commune so that whatever the laws dictate might be done.

The events of February 1792 and February 1793 provide insight into the complex ways in which Parisian *femmes sans-culottes* worked within and on the margins of revolutionary institutions, fusing tactics like petitioning, which they had mastered and practiced within their popular societies, Section assemblies, and as members of organized trades, with *taxation populaire*, insurrectionary demands invoking the people's right to subsistence commodities at a just price.

The response of authorities to the feminine politics of violence changed over the course of the year. In February 1792, the Legislative Assembly listened to reports by the mayor of Paris on popular disturbances. The mayor told the deputies that he had confronted the protesting crowds, who assured him that they were not gathered to pillage. The mayor suggested that they try petitioning, and they did. The Legislative Assembly blamed counterrevolutionary hoarders for inciting the people, but recommended nothing more than voluntary boycotts of colonial products. The following year, the National Convention again blamed the popular violence on aristocrats, but moved beyond calls for voluntary abstinence to vote new sums of money to the Commune for provisioning

Paris. The Convention also authorized the municipality to sound the general alarm; one deputy, Chaumette, urged laws against hoarders and regulations governing the issuing of *assignats* [Paper certificates backed by confiscated ecclesiastical or aristocratic property]. He insisted that wages must be coordinated with the price of necessities if liberty was to mean anything at all to poor people.

In the popular societies, Section assemblies, and radical clubs where women of the people frequently gathered – as members or as spectators – during the radical phase of the revolution (1793–1794), leadership and control had typically devolved to their friends, brothers, fathers, and husbands, an articulate *sans-culotte* elite. It was not, however, until February 1793, at a critical stage in the power struggle pitting Girondin moderates against Jacobin radicals, that the common women of Paris succeeded in establishing their own institutional base, the Society of Revolutionary Republican Women. The society allowed for the most complete institutionalization of the *femmes sans-culottes*' revolutionary political activity. The society had its own regulations, with carefully elaborated procedures for meeting, for election of officers, for membership, correspondence, and deputations. It had its own meeting place. The society's known leaders, Pauline Léon and Claire Lacombe, were women with socially marginal occupations; Léon was a chocolate-maker, a trade undermined by sugar shortages and the departure of the aristocrats, and Lacombe was an actress from the provinces. Both had been active in revolutionary events before 1793. Perhaps most central to their real influence on revolutionary politics was their close contacts and effective working alliances within Sections controlled by *sans-culottes*. They formed a close liaison with the *Enragés*, spokesmen on the far left for the *sans-culottes*' interests. The Revolutionary Republicans had proven their loyalty to the Jacobins during the critical journées of May–June 1793; they joined with Jacobins, Section chiefs and residents, the National Guard, members of popular societies, and *Engragés* to oust Girondin deputies from the Convention. They also enjoyed important contacts with the Cordeliers Club.

By September 1793, the society, which numbered several hundred members, campaigned actively for the implementation of a political program which the Montagnard establishment, along with market women and even some members of the society itself, found massively threatening.

In the autumn of 1793, the society, in combination with the *Enragés* and other radical democratic factions, applied heavy pressure on Sections, popular societies, Jacobin clubs, and Convention deputies to support a full program of protective and repressive measures for the safety of the people. Their tactic paid off. The Convention legalized the Terror on September 5; voted an *armée révolutionnaire* on the ninth; passed a law of suspects on the seventeenth. On the twenty-ninth, the Convention passed a law of the 'general maximum', providing for uniform price controls on necessities. On September 21, again acceding to pressure from the society, the Convention voted to require all women to wear the revolutionary tricolor cockade in public. The society's members were aggressive and relentless in pressing the revolutionary authorities to enforce this legislation energetically.

Despite these efforts, the society met with defeat, defeat at the hands of Montagnards as well as women in the district where the society was holding its meetings. Market women, former servants, and religious women opposed the price controls the society supported and were critical of legislation meting out harsh punishments for suspect aristocrats and former clergy. They resisted the new legislation on the tricolor cockade. Even more critical, Montagnard authorities at all levels were also threatened by the Revolutionary Republicans. Along with the *Enragés*, the society's members represented the most coherent opposition in revolutionary Paris to critical proposals in the Montagnard political program. The society was one of the very few remaining fighting fronts for a *sans-culotte* population which persisted in waging war for the complete realization of a democratic society of liberty, equality, fraternity, and virtue.

The Revolutionary Republicans conspicuously opposed Jacobin policies of compromise with moderate revolutionaries whose support, in fact, the Jacobins needed to supply the armies and to maintain themselves in power. The women relentlessly exposed the Jacobins' unfulfilled constitutional promises; they demanded enforcement of the law of the general maximum, the surveillance of merchants, and the use of *sans-culotte* vigilante forces to control revolutionary officials. On September 16, 1793, at a meeting of the Jacobin Society, members who a few weeks earlier had offered the Society of Revolutionary Republican Women its meeting hall, greeted its deputations warmly, and supported its members' views on terror and subsistence, exposed and denounced the Revolutionary Republican leader Claire Lacombe along with Théophile Leclerc, the *Enragé* journalist. The Jacobins charged that Républicaines-Révolutionnaires had spoken scornfully of 'M. Robespierre who dared to treat them as counter-revolutionaries'; one member reported that 'Citoyenne Lacombe meddles everywhere'; at one assembly meeting, 'she asked for the constitution, the whole constitution, only the constitution ... after which she wanted to sap the foundation of the constitution and overturn all kinds of constituted authorities'; motions were entertained which would have called for the revolutionary women to 'rid themselves by a purifying vote of the suspect women who control the Society' and requesting that word be sent to the Committee of General Security to 'have suspect women arrested'; first of all Citoyenne Lacombe. In the end, Lacombe did appear before the Committee of General Security; her papers were sealed, but when inspected, were found to contain no incriminating evidence.

In October 1793, when the Républicaines-Révolutionnaires attempted to enforce the law on the cockade, outraged and threatened market women attacked the society's members in the streets. At the end of October – newly dated 7 Brumaire, Year II – market women, aided and abetted by hostile authorities, stormed a meeting of the Revolutionary Republicans and abused and beat society members with impunity. When the society's vice-president called upon the Section Revolutionary Committee to draw up a *procès-verbal* of the incident, the committee deliberately delayed; women suspected of assault and battery were brought to the committee, but they were released. When the Revolutionary Republicans persisted in their demands for a *procès-verbal*, a troop officer, in collusion with committee members, persuaded them to desist, to abandon their *procès-verbal*, and to make their escape from what the officer falsely assured them was a huge, angry crowd crying 'Vive la République! Down with the *révolutionnaires!*'

The following day, 8 Brumaire, a delegation of market women filed a formal complaint against the Revolutionary Republican Women with the Convention. And on the ninth André Amar reported to the Convention on behalf of the Committee of General Security.

He questioned the patriotism of the Républicaines-Révolutionnaires, intimating that they were counterrevolutionaries. He went further, addressing himself to two general considerations: 'Should women exercise political rights and meddle in affairs of government?' and 'Should women meet in political associations? ... Can women devote themselves to these useful and difficult functions?'. His answer was that women were physiologically, psychologically, and intellectually incapable of governing.

One deputy asked whether it made sense to invoke higher principles to justify dissolving popular societies, even if it could be shown that some members had committed indiscretions. Another deputy argued that the Convention had already 'thrown a veil over principles out of fear that they might be abused to lead us into counter-revolution. Therefore, it is only a question of knowing whether women's societies are dangerous.' The Convention decreed: 'The National Convention after having heard the report of its Committee of General Security, decrees: Article 1: Clubs and popular societies of women, whatever name they are known under, are prohibited [Article] 2: All sessions of popular societies must be public.'

When women appeared at the Convention during a session of 15 Brumaire with a petition protesting the radical revolutionary leadership's liquidation of the Society of Revolutionary Republican Women, the deputies refused to hear them: 'The women petitioners leave the bar hurriedly', the *Moniteur* reported. When a deputation of women wearing the red caps of the Revolutionary Republicans appeared before the General Council of the Paris Commune on 27 Brumaire, Chaumette, a council member who had tangled earlier with the Revolutionary Republicans, reminded the deputation that physiological and cultural considerations indicated to women: 'Be a woman. The tender cares owing to infancy, household details, the sweet anxieties of maternity, these are your labors.' Chaumette also reminded the petitioners of the fate of La Roland and 'the impudent Olympe de Gouges who was the first to set up women's societies, who abandoned the cares of her household to get mixed up in the republic and whose head fell beneath the avenging knife of the laws. Is it the place of women to propose motions? Is it the place of women to place themselves at the head of our armies?' Chaumette's demand that the woman's deputation not be heard, that no future female deputation be received, except on an ad hoc basis, was warmly applauded and unanimously adopted.

The Revolutionary Republicans institutionalized political roles for *femmes sans-culottes* more fully and more successfully than any other body in revolutionary Paris. Radical revolutionary authorities responsible for repressing this society, whose leaders and members had crystallized and successfully implemented a political program to satisfy the needs of the *menu peuple* for protection and subsistence, had taken a fateful step that would lead inexorably to the liquidation of the organizational bases for the democratic revolution in Paris.

By the time that Robespierre and the Montagnards proclaimed the revolutionary government on October 30, 1793, a day after the dissolution of the Society of Revolutionary Republican Women, they had undermined the political power of the *Enragés* and the Revolutionary Republicans, among the last groups capable of exerting programmatic efforts on behalf of the common people. The Jacobins did not want to risk being exposed by organized censors and critics continually demanding that they fulfill their constitutional guarantees and promises. Women did continue to contact authorities but generally to petition for the satisfaction of personal demands and not to represent larger issues, in part because the organizational bases from which such confrontations would normally come had been eroded by the government of the Terror. During the Terror, wives petitioned on behalf of husbands in the army or in jail; teachers asked for help in collecting unpaid salaries; workers attested to the revolutionary patriotism of their employers. Despite the problems of provisioning the city in wartime, the Montagnards maintained steady, reassuring supplies of subsistence goods at controlled prices.

In July 1794, government authority shifted suddenly back to better-off people – the Thermidorians – who undermined both the political institutions which had given power to the *menu peuple* and the economic legislation which had protected their livelihood. In October 1794 new laws prohibited petitions, affiliations, and correspondence among clubs. Price supports were curtailed in favor of free trade, which brought back hoarding, speculation, and inflation – and food shortages and long bread lines. The last great popular revolutionary insurrections, the *journées* of Germinal and Prairial, broke out in response to these deprivations. Over a three-month period, in a series of collisions with authorities, women once again used the strategies which they had mastered in the course of the Revolution. They led protest marches, they carried petitions to the Section committees and the National Convention; and they engaged in their traditional *taxation populaire*. However, they operated without benefit of formalized revolutionary organizations: popular societies, sympathetic Section officials, and strategic allies among journalists and deputies. The organization they could use was conspiratorial. When these conspiracies were uncovered, women who had further strategies at hand had no option except to submit.

Interrogations and police reports show that the authorities felt threatened by calls for a return of the institutions that had been the bases of popular influence the previous year. One witness during a police interrogation on the night of 29 Germinal recalled overhearing the remarks of a woman during a conversation on a street corner: 'Yes. I see women who, when they receive a quarter-pound loaf, not having gotten any the night before, are really satisfied and very happy. If you go to present a petition about it to the National Convention, you are arrested. The popular societies have been closed. That was in order to plunge us back into slavery. We are all suckers'.

Officials also feared crowds of women as the most serious threat to public order. For example, on 7 Floréal, Year III, a police investigator reporting on 'the mood of the public' stated:

> The women, above all, seemed to be playing the principal role there [in the squares, streets, public places, and at the bakers']; they were taunting the men, treating them as cowards and seemed unwilling to be satisfied with the portion that was offered to them. A large number of them wanted to rush into insurrection; even the majority appeared to be determined to attack the constituted authorities and notably the government Comités, which would have happened were it not for the prudence and firmness of the armed troops.

Women led marches from Section headquarters to the Convention, mobilizing women along the route; they seized flour wagons, violently protested to the Comité civil that they would not allow the flour to be distributed to the bakers; in the end they took the law into their own hands, arresting members of the Comité civil 'in the name of the sovereign people'.

Finally, it required an armed force from the Section, reinforced by troops from other Sections, to end the disturbance.

After 1795, Parisian women did not again rise in insurrection until 1848. We want to question whether there is any progression in the nature, extent, and significance of female political participation moving from the spring of 1789 to the spring of 1795.

Women began as subjects who reacted to elite initiatives by zealously guarding traditional prerogatives, but they learned to operate as citizens working through revolutionary institutions to demand the satisfaction of needs as rights which were abstract and sophisticated and which included political power. Real life seldom progresses with theoretical neatness, but there is documentary evidence for such a transition. This essay is concerned not only with describing how women came to work through organizations for revolutionary goals, but also with explaining why they did so and whether their efforts had political significance. Such an explanation must link the nature of people's demands, the collective actions they take, the organizational bases from which they operate, and the responses of governmental authorities.

In the late summer of 1789, the processions of women in Paris represent a fascinating mix of traditional harvest festival and a show of force by a vigilant citizenry. During the October Days, women demonstrated to demand that the king resume his medieval role as provider, but their actions imply a vague recognition of current political issues, such as the royal veto clause in the Constitution and the roles of deputies as representatives of the popular will. This awareness increased as revolutionary activists published journals, harangued public gatherings, and founded clubs and popular societies. The petition on royal executive powers of July 1791 represents many of the elements of modern collective political action: a deliberate, planned gathering on the Champ de Mars, petitions to the Jacobins and the National Assembly spelling out specific demands for a referendum, and the participation of organized associational groups, including the Cordeliers. The demonstration lacked tight organization and control. The violent retaliation by authorities, coupled with the Assembly's restoration of full executive authority to the king, ended any further large-scale collective action until the sugar crisis of February 1792.

The food riots of 1792 and 1793 differed in scale and in the reaction of authorities. Both represented, again, a mix of traditional ad hoc demands that government protect the food supply and participatory tactics of petitioning local and national government. By 1793 protesters were adding demands for permanent protection, enforceable laws against hoarding, and the regulation of currency.

The activities and tactics of the Républicaines-Révolutionnaires are indications that women had come to understand how to corner a share of political power: purging the Convention, policing the markets, arguing for the harsh prosecution of suspects, petitioning for specific laws to control the marketplace both economically and physically.

In the spring of 1793, women had linked their subsistence grievances to their constitutional rights. What is striking in these events is the evidence of the authorities' tactics of relying upon neighborhood groups to control behavior by using spies, setting tradeswomen against their customers, or urging men and women in street gatherings or bread lines to implicate one another.

Clearly, the popular associational institutions such as Section assemblies of the Year II and popular societies were not sufficiently large, tightly organized, or supported to prevent the Thermidorians from using centralized and controlled police networks and local and national government to destroy the women's political power.

Female political leaders often emerged from marginal social positions – actresses, former practitioners of the undermined luxury trades – or from occupations such as printing and publishing that put them at the center of political communication. When dramatic events, uncertain power struggles, or economic scarcity were great enough, as in the summer of 1791 and the spring of 1793, more women became involved. Women signed petitions, marched and demonstrated, attended meetings, formed deputations, and persuaded, frightened, or coerced political authorities to accede to their demands. When police and other agents of government threatened them, or when they felt their security undermined by aristocrats, hoarders, and speculators, they joined forces in popular societies and Section assemblies.

The crucial variable determining the nature and extent of women's political influence is the availability of political institutions geographically proximate, sympathetic to women's interests, and open to women as spectators, petitioners, delegates, and members. Women who had earlier joined up with loosely organized and somewhat incoherent groups rooted in the parish, the market, and the trade and occupational structures in Paris were able to move during the revolutionary mobilization into popular societies, the Section assemblies, and the galleries of the Commune and the national legislatures. These popular organizations did not last sufficiently long to enable their participants to overcome their rivalries and to integrate their interests. Government officials were aware of these rivalries and exploited them, in addition to using tactics of repression, to regain and perpetuate control over the city. Two generations later, the granddaughters of the women of the Revolution would emulate them as heroines, remembering that they had been among those who began the fight for popular control of political power.

What is unique about the French Revolution, compared to other revolutions in the eighteenth-century world, is that it was a democratic revolution which not only enlightened but engaged an entire nation of French men and French women in the struggle for influence and power as citizen participants. Government repression, targeting *femmes sans-culottes* – sometimes along with men and sometimes as especially threatening insurgents – brought this democratic experiment to an end.

---

[1] All eighteenth-century documents quoted in English in this extract are the authors' translations, cited from their book with Mary D. Johnson, *Women in Revolutionary Paris, 1789–1795*, (Urbana, University of Illinois Press, 1979).

A22 François Furet and Denis Richet, Introductory section to 'The New France'

From F. Furet and D. Richet (1965) *French Revolution*, Paris, English translation by Stephen Hardman (1970) New York.

During the Directory, when the bloodbaths of the Terror had become a thing of the past, French society began to reveal the profound changes brought about by the Revolution, changes which gave that society an essentially modern character. At the collapse of the Old Regime, the phenomenon of the 'natural' family, with its high birth- and mortality-rates, had already ceased to exist. But a study of population figures for eighteenth-century France suggests a particularly sharp drop in the birth-rate for the decade 1790–1800: according to the census of 1792 and 1793, for example, there were three hundred and eighty-four births per hundred marriages, compared with four hundred and seventy-six for the period 1778–87. The difference between these figures is all the more significant because during the Revolution the average age at marriage was lower than it had been under the Old Regime.

As variations in population trends inevitably have a delayed effect, French society in the latter years of the eighteenth century did not suffer the consequences of its lower birth-rate; on the contrary, benefiting from the high birth-rate and reduced mortality-rate which had been characteristic of the century, France still had the largest population of any country in Europe and was therefore able to continue supplying men for the armies of revolutionary expansionism. But the fall in the birth-rate in the last ten years of the century points to a fundamental change in the mental climate of France, for it surely suggests a greater control of sexual behaviour and the rapid development of contraceptive techniques. Contraception had undoubtedly been practised for some considerable time among the educated classes and had become more widespread as living standards improved during the second half of the century; in the reigns of both Louis XV and Louis XVI demographers and moralists were already deploring its harmful effects, which they exaggerated. It seems, however, that contraception was not practised generally in France until the Revolution, indicating a profound break with the religious prohibitions of the past and a new attitude towards human values and happiness. In France, the Malthusian Revolution had no chronological correlation with the Industrial Revolution, as it had in the other great countries of Europe. This demonstrated that France was more advanced intellectually than economically.

The new trend was not only a sign of a secularised world; it was very much a part of the new France of the property-owners, men anxious to have smaller families so that each of their children would have the best possible chance of success in life. Property-ownership spread rapidly during the Revolution with the sale of nationalised land, especially in the rural areas. Georges Lefebvre has estimated that in northern France a third of the thirty thousand peasants who bought nationalised lands during the period of the Revolution had possessed nothing before 1789. Many peasants began their slow and painstaking accumulation of wealth by purchasing small plots of ground, just like old Grandet in Balzac's novel.

The spread of property-ownership in the towns is more difficult to assess statistically, but it was no less real: during the hard times of economic and financial crisis, a petty bourgeoisie of tradesmen and craftsmen had grown up; at the same time, the Revolution had brought a vast increase in the numbers of public officials and the abolition of venal offices had made positions in public service open to all. Though lawyers were less wealthy than they had been under Louis XVI and many *rentiers* were totally ruined, bourgeois France had begun to assume some of its essentially modern features. The country was becoming increasingly dominated by the wealth of the merchant and the tradesman and the political power of the deputy. Now that the barriers of social privilege had been swept away, an egalitarian society was slowly taking shape, a society in which opportunities for advancement depended largely on individual talent, the hazards of financial speculation and the vicissitudes of political life. And yet the new France resembled the old in more ways than men believed. The social pleasures of the Directory were not so very different from those of the Old Regime, and it was no mere coincidence that during these years Talleyrand regained some of his former zest for life.

Perhaps it is misleading to define a society by concentrating on its most dazzling features. After all, French society in the years following the First World War was not just the Paris of Cocteau. Similarly, in the period of the Directory, when Mme Tallien reigned supreme over all Paris, the Grandets of rural France were amassing their fortunes so that they could make their sons into 'messieurs'. But modern social history, in its concern with detailed statistics, is in danger of attaching too little importance to the Parisian scene which the Goncourts described so vividly. During the Directory, Paris finally established itself in the role of pre-eminence prepared for it by the intelligentsia and salons of the eighteenth century, a role in which it had already distinguished itself as the centre of all the great events of the Revolution. Versailles was now deserted, no more than a memory: the City had won its struggle against the Court. Paris and power were henceforth inseparable. At first the capital had used its newly-found supremacy as an instrument of terror. Now, with the years of tragedy past, it inherited the status that had formerly belonged to the court at Versailles: it became the centre of money, of women and of pleasure, the symbol of the ideal life of which provincial France dreamed.

The money spent on dining and entertaining in Paris belonged to a new class of rich men, for most of the wealth of the Old Regime had been plundered by the Terror and inflation. But fortunes were still built up in much the same way, by traditional methods of speculative trading, and in particular by taking advantage of the chaotic state of the Treasury, rather than by the profit-based methods of modern capitalism. The contractors of the Republic proved even more unscrupulous than their ancestors, the Farmers General of the Old Regime. The increase in public expenditure, the necessity of providing for the armies, the inefficiency of the tax-collecting system and monetary instability had created ideal conditions for speculation and profiteering of every kind; an oligarchy of financiers guaranteed the Treasury's debts and took a large part of the nation's wealth as security. Starting from nothing, these men set no limit to their ambitions, for they had no one to fear: in former times the king of France had wielded an authority over his creditors which the Republic could not possibly hope to emulate. Politics and finance had become more closely interdependent: Barras and Ouvrard were the first two representatives of the new alliance.

However, the money that was being made so easily and rapidly was not diverted into the productive fields of investment and savings; preserving its old aristocratic function, wealth was devoted to the pursuit of pleasure, as if the new society of bourgeois France unconsciously hoped to endow itself with the aura of nobility. Pleasure is not acquired as easily as power, and the bourgeoisie of the Directory could find no other way of enjoying itself than imitating the social habits of the Old Regime. But the setting had changed, for the great houses of the Faubourg Saint-Germain were now deserted or had been sold and the social life of the city had moved across to the right bank, where public dances had replaced the private functions of earlier days. Nearly all the most distinguished figures of the old society were abroad or in the provinces, although a few returned to Paris where they were welcomed in the more snobbish circles. The new society already had in its midst a number of deserters from the aristocracy who were able to set an example to the rest; men like Barras himself, formerly a viscount and now an irremovable Director, the new regent of a kingless France; and Talleyrand, the 'bishop' who had returned from America.

The frenzied cult of pleasure was not just a reaction against the puritan repression of the years of the Terror; it also expressed a yearning for social vengeance. When Bonaparte married Josephine de Beauharnais, whose name evoked an aristocratic past, he acted not as a vulgar opportunist, but as a man passionately in love who wanted to obliterate memories of a humiliated childhood. Thus women occupied an even more dominant position in the society of the Directory than under the Old Regime; they were the incarnation not only of pleasure and luxury, but of money and success. During the years which separated the religious and social prohibitions of the Old Regime and the restrictive severity of the Civil Code, women enjoyed a brief emancipation, revelling in the homage which the new society paid to feminine beauty and draping their bodies in scanty pseudo-classical garments. The astute Josephine, well aware of the passing of time and of youth, took many lovers who helped her to climb to the top ranks of society. She provided the link between the Revolution and the Empire. The true queen of Paris was Mme Tallien, a woman of sculptural beauty and the mistress of both Barras and Ouvrard. A ball without her was unthinkable.

The men who enjoyed the limelight in the society of the Directory were the intellectuals and the military. Here again, although the new revolutionary society had either destroyed the flower of the old nobility or driven it from the country, it had inherited the institutions of the old order: Sieyès and Bonaparte replaced Turgot and Choiseul as France's leading figures in the academic and military worlds. But the new men of France were much more powerful than their counterparts of the Old Regime had ever been. The jurists of royal absolutism had merely been clerks, but the deputies of the Revolution wielded vast powers; the king's marshals had hardly been more than courtiers, while the generals of the Republic were great liberating heroes. Liberty and military conquest had made all things possible. Money certainly played an open part in the political life of the Directory, but it did not rule supreme. The Revolution had reinforced an unwritten law of French history whereby businessmen refrain from taking part personally in the struggle for power.

The Terror had been the regime of the intellectuals and the *sans-culottes*. The Directory was the republic of the academics and the generals. From the newly-founded Institute, and through the medium of secondary and higher education, the ideologists of the Directory spread the message of the eighteenth-century Enlightenment over bourgeois France. Voltaire, Condillac and Condorcet came into their own; their aim had been to banish superstition by education and to establish society on rational foundations. The Enlightenment now exercised greater influence over France than at any other period of the Revolution, and its ambition was to uproot the Church and put natural religion in its place. Much of modern France was born of these Utopian ideals and the upheavals which issued from them. But the national consciousness forged by the intellectuals of the Revolution was inevitably Messianic in character, for the banner of Enlightenment had become the banner of the French armies beyond the Rhine and the Alps. Thus the revolutionary war continued to perform the role invented for it by the Girondins, endowing the French soldier with the twofold prestige of arms and ideas. Victorious generals contributed more to the Republic's ideology than to its coffers. Yet their view of the Republic was less academic and less bourgeois than that of the intellectuals: they looked on France as the people itself, all that was durable amid the ephemeral victories of politicians.

The way in which Parisian society abandoned itself wholly to the world of pleasure and entertainment was also a sign of its uncertainty with regard to the future. Since the execution of the king of France the Revolution had not been able to put in his place a political authority acceptable to the country as a whole. The Republic of Enlightenment preached by the academics of the Institute had no deep roots among the French people. It was still confronted by its natural adversaries, the Church and the royalists, more united than ever by the persecution they had suffered together. On the other hand, the Republic was finding increasing difficulty in uniting those who had benefited from the Revolution: many peasants, even those who had bought national land, still preferred to listen to their priest and resisted the attempts made by the bourgeois of the towns to substitute the new religion for their traditional Catholic faith. Moreover, while clerical control of primary education had been destroyed by abolishing all the Old Regime's country schools where children had been taught to read and write from holy books, the Republic had put nothing in their place; concentrating its attention entirely on secondary and higher education, on the towns and the children of the bourgeoisie, it had no alternative system of education to offer the inhabitants of rural France. The peasant, whose horizon extended no further than his slightly enlarged plot of land, still feared the return of the landowners of the Old Regime and wanted firmer guarantees of security than the endless *coups d'état* in Paris could provide. Naturally mistrustful of his deputy and a prisoner of the monarchic tradition of power, the peasant would have liked to see what Mirabeau and so many others had longed for since 1789: a king committed to the Revolution.

This was also the wish of many of the bourgeoisie who were looking for a new, conservative regime. After all the years of inflation, war and upheavals of various kinds, stability had become the dream of 1798, just as change had been the dream of 1789. This is always a sign that a revolution has succeeded.

Post-Revolutionary Society

Revolutionary France had inherited the passion of the eighteenth century for taking censuses. Questionnaires and inquiries, similar to those undertaken by Louis XVI's intendants, were conducted all over the country, so that it is possible to make a statistical comparison of population figures for the Old Regime and the period of the Revolution. In the spring of 1796 the Directory received a long report on the population of France which had been drawn up by the great mathematician Prony, who at the time was head of the surveying and planning department. In his calculations Prony had followed the common practice of basing censuses on the boundaries of Old France, though he had extended these a little to include Avignon, Comtat, Savoy and the Maritime Alps. He had imitated the method employed by Terray's and Necker's intendants, basing his figures on the average number of annual births. By this method he obtained a total of 28 million inhabitants. The national almanac for Year IV gave a total of 27.8 millions

(31.8 millions including the Belgian departments, 32.9 millions including the colonies).

The France of the Directory was still one of the most densely populated countries in Europe, and showed no signs of the supposed effects of depopulation which the enemies of the Revolution had attributed to the war, emigration and, above all, the Terror. The most recent estimates put the total number of emigrés at one hundred and fifty thousand and the total for the guillotine's victims at about twenty thousand; moreover, in the eighteenth century the death-toll of war, both civil and foreign, was infinitely less than it has been in the present century. The figures just given are statistically insignificant when set against the general trend towards population-growth which was characteristic of the second half of the eighteenth century in France. The population of France in 1789 was about twenty-six millions; by 1795 the total for the same area (i.e. within the boundaries of 1789) was about twenty-seven and a half millions.

France remained essentially a rural nation, and towns of over two thousand inhabitants accounted for less than one-fifth of the total population. France recruited her armies fom the peasantry; since the beginning of the Revolution over eight hundred and fifty thousand men had entered military service. The size of France's population was one of the keys to the course taken by the Revolution, and to Napoleon's rise to power.

A young Burgundian noble lady who had been imprisoned during the Terror, Mme de Chastenay, came back to Paris to spend the winter of 1796–7 with friends. She was to remember those months for the rest of her life:

> Never had winter in Paris been so gay. As in the provinces, all the best people gathered at the subscription balls. All over France the pleasures of life were cultivated quite uninhibitedly. A long period of famine had come to an end, money had reappeared and with it an abundance of everything. The revolutionary regime was over once and for all. No-one now spoke of informers or gendarmes. I have never seen people enjoying themselves as much as this; masks were even worn on the highways – life was just one great carnival.

The eighteenth century had returned to France, with its masks, its merrymaking and its women. But Mme de Chastenay was too young to recognise that these were different faces concealed beneath the masks and different women reigning over a new society. The aristocracy of eighteenth-century France had passed on its social customs to the upstarts of the Revolution, and was now horrified to see this distorted and yet somehow faithful reflection of itself in the people's mad rush to indulge in pleasures once reserved for the privileged few.

A23 Matthew Anderson, Introduction to *The Ascendancy of Europe, 1815–1914* (a summary of the period 1780s–1815)

From M.S. Anderson, (1985) *The Ascendancy of Europe, 1815–1914,* 2nd edn, Longman.

The generation or more which separates the 1780s from the battle of Waterloo saw the beginnings of modern history in Europe. During the eighteenth century the continent was still, in its everyday life, closer to the twelfth century than to the twentieth. Economic change, though real and important, was by the standards of succeeding generations very slow. Though there was a remarkable growth of population, industrial organization remained for the greater part highly traditional. Technology, largely unaffected by scientific discovery, advanced erratically and at no great speed. As late as 1776 Adam Smith could tacitly assume, in his *Wealth of Nations*, that the economies of the European states were static, or growing only very slowly. Society continued almost everywhere to be, as it had been for centuries, a complex network of groups often enjoying, by law or tradition, important corporate privileges – village communities, guilds, towns, churches, even universities. It was still, over much of the continent, divided into traditional 'orders' – Church, nobility, burghers, peasantry – whose members enjoyed different legal rights, bore different legal burdens and possessed different legal personalities.

The governments of continental Europe before the French Revolution, with a few rather unimportant exceptions, were, as they had been for generations, monarchies of a more or less absolute kind. It is true that absolutism was now being changed and tempered by new forces. 'Enlightened despots', inspired largely by the example and success of Frederick II of Prussia, began to pride themselves on working for (though hardly ever with) their peoples, and as a rule accepted the idea that they and their subjects were bound together by some vague form of quasi-contractual relationship. Moreover the commercial, naval and colonial successes achieved by Britain had now made ideas of limited and parliamentary monarchy more acceptable than ever before, at least in parts of western Europe. The monarchical mystique was thus less pervasive and demanding than in the seventeenth century; the two or three generations before the French Revolution produced no Bossuet. None the less no major continental state possessed in the 1780s an effective parliament; and republicanism was a remote classical tradition, a piece of political antiquarianism rather than a living idea. Even the armed forces of which rulers made use in the furtherance of their territorial disputes and dynastic claims were highly traditional. The sailing man-of-war armed with smooth-bore cannon using crude black gunpowder had not changed in essentials for well over two centuries: armies were relatively small and often dynastic rather than national in their outlook.

By 1815 this traditional structure had changed almost beyond recognition over much of western Europe and had been seriously shaken in central Europe. This dramatic change was the work in part of the British example. Britain's wealth, her ability to sustain unflinchingly an unprecedentedly expensive and difficult struggle with France which dragged on for more than two decades (1793–1814, with an interval of fourteen months from March 1802 to May 1803) were a spectacular advertisement for industrialization and parliamentary government. But incomparably more important in precipitating change was the challenge and later the overwhelming threat of revolutionary France. The Declaration of the Rights of Man of August 1789, and the spirit which it embodied, made impossible the continuance in France of a society based on inequalities sanctified by law. They also aroused over much of Europe, at least among the educated, intense admiration and genuine sympathy. A vast wave of constructive change in France during the two or three years which followed – the ending of feudalism, the reform of local government, the sweeping away of internal barriers to trade and of obstructive corporate bodies such as the *parlements* and the guilds, the new moderate monarchical constitution of 1791 – seemed to radicals and idealists everywhere to point the way forward to the rest of Europe and to show that the traditional mould of government and society could be broken. The idea that a people, independent of or even against the wishes of its rulers, could and must control its own destiny, the alluring and potentially very dangerous belief that no established right had any validity against the popular will, had now been asserted with exciting and terrifying force.

The revolutionaries were not content to preach merely by example. By the spring of 1792 the increasingly messianic tone of the revolution, coupled with the complexities of the struggle for power in Paris, had led to the outbreak of war between France and the powers of the old Europe. In 1793–94 the threat of foreign invasion and civil war established in France, though for little more than a year, the Jacobin dictatorship which was for a century to symbolize for most Europeans the cruelty and terror of revolution. From the brief and violent life of this régime was to spring one of the most powerful and durable of all political myths, a grim warning to many and a glowing inspiration to few for generations to come. The drive towards genuine social and economic change, always a minor aspect of the Jacobin régime, was decisively defeated in 1794–95; and this defeat was driven home by the seizure of power by General Bonaparte in 1799. But however conservative the social outlook of the Emperor Napoleon I (as he became in 1804), he represented to the full the expansionist tendencies which had shown themselves in France from 1792 onwards. Under him the sheer military power of the country, based ultimately on its great superiority in population to almost all other European states, appeared to threaten the permanent subordination of most of the continent to French rule. For a decade or more he seemed to have overthrown the balance of power, perhaps for ever. The Habsburg Empire, Prussia, to a lesser extent even Russia, all fell before him in the campaigns of 1805–07; and the years 1807–10, when his empire in Europe was at its height, saw his power apparently beyond challenge. His own lack of moderation and statesmanship destroyed that power in 1812–14. But his career had shown with frightening clarity the potentialities of the new forces – the impatience of traditional restraints, the demand for a more fluid type of society and for more rational and effective government – released by the revolution in France.

The Europe of 1815 was thus a continent in some ways and in some areas (above all east of a line from Hamburg to the head of the Adriatic and south of the Alps and the Pyrenees) still traditional, but one struggling to come to terms with a series of challenging and indeed revolutionary forces. Industrialism, mass conscript armies, reformed and rationalized bureaucracies, most of all the new and dynamic political ideals of popular sovereignty and national self-determination spread by the revolution in France, were beginning to transform the old Europe of monarchs, landed nobilities, often unfree peasants, the Europe of tradition, privilege and ancestral pieties. By 1914 that transformation was far advanced. The story of its advance is the theme of this book.

Section B PHILOSOPHY: ROUSSEAU

B1 Rousseau, *The Social Contract*, extract from bk4, ch.8, 'On Civil Religion'

From Donald A. Cress (ed.) (1987) *Jean-Jacques Rousseau: The Basic Political Writings*, Indianapolis, Hackett, pp.224–7.

Thus there remains the religion of man or Christianity (not that of today, but that of the Gospel, which is completely different). Through this holy, sublime, true religion, men, in being the children of the same God, all acknowledge one another as brothers, and the society that unites them is not dissolved even at death.

But since this religion has no particular relation to the body politic, it leaves laws with only the force the laws derive from themselves, without adding any other force to them. And thus one of the great bonds of a particular society remains ineffectual. Moreover, far from attaching the hearts of the citizens to the state, it detaches them from it as from all the other earthly things. I know of nothing more contrary to the social spirit.

We are told that a people of true Christians would form the most perfect society imaginable. I see but one major difficulty in this assumption, namely that a society of true Christians would no longer be a society of men.

I even say that this supposed society would not, for all its perfection, be the strongest or the most durable. By dint of being perfect, it would lack a bond of union; its destructive vice would be in its very perfection.

Each man would fulfill his duty; the people would be subject to the laws; the leaders would be just and moderate, the magistrates would be upright and incorruptible; soldiers would scorn death; there would be neither vanity nor luxury. All of this is very fine, but let us look further.

Christianity is a completely spiritual religion, concerned exclusively with things heavenly. The homeland of the Christian is not of this world. He does his duty, it is true, but he does it with a profound indifference toward the success or failure of his efforts. So long as he has nothing to reproach himself for, it matters little to him whether anything is going well or poorly down here. If the state is flourishing, he hardly dares to enjoy the public felicity, for fear of becoming puffed up with his country's glory. If the state is in decline, he blesses the hand of God that weighs heavily on his people.

For the society to be peaceful and for harmony to be maintained, every citizen without exception would have to be an equally good Christian. But if, unhappily, there is a single ambitious man, a single hypocrite, a Cataline, for example, or a Cromwell, he would quite undoubtedly gain the upper hand on his pious compatriots. Christian charity does not readily allow one to think ill of his neighbors. Once he has discovered by some ruse the art of deceiving them and of laying hold of a part of the public authority, behold a man established in dignity! God wills that he be respected. Soon, behold a power! God wills that he be obeyed. Does the trustee of his power abuse it? He is the rod with which God punishes his children. It would be against one's conscience to expel the usurper. It would be necessary to disturb the public tranquillity, use violence and shed blood. All this accords ill with the meekness of a Christian. And after all, what difference does it make whether one is a free man or a serf in this vale of tears? The essential thing is getting to heaven, and resignation is but another means to that end.

What if a foreign war breaks out? The citizens march without reservation into combat; none among them dreams of deserting. They do their duty, but without passion for victory; they know how to die better than how to be victorious. What difference does it make whether they are the victors or the vanquished? Does not providence know better than they what they need? Just imagine the advantage a fierce, impetuous and passionate enemy could draw from their stoicism! Set them face to face with those generous peoples who were devoured by an ardent love of glory and homeland. Suppose your Christian republic is face to face with Sparta or Rome. The pious Christians will be beaten, crushed and destroyed before they realize where they are, or else they will owe their safety only to the scorn their enemies will conceive for them. To my way of thinking, the oath taken by Fabius' soldiers was a fine one. They did not swear to die or to win; they swore to return victorious. And they kept their promise. Christians would never have taken such an oath; they would have believed they were tempting God.

But I am deceiving myself in talking about a Christian republic; these terms are mutually exclusive. Christianity preaches only servitude and dependence. Its spirit is too favorable to tyranny for tyranny not to take advantage of it at all times. True Christians are made to be slaves. They know it and are hardly moved by this. This brief life has too little value in their eyes.

Christian troops, we are told, are excellent. I deny this. Is someone going to show me some? For my part, I do not know of any Christian troops. Someone will mention the crusades. Without disputing the valor of the crusaders, I will point out that quite far from being Christians, they were soldiers of the priest; they were citizens of the church; they were fighting for its spiritual country which the church, God knows how, had made temporal. Properly understood, this is a throwback to paganism. Since the Gospel does not establish a national religion, no holy war is possible among Christians.

Under the pagan emperors, Christian soldiers were brave. All the Christian authors affirm this, and I believe it. This was a competition for honor against the pagan troops. Once the emperors were Christians, this competition ceased. And when the cross expelled the eagle, all Roman valor disappeared.

But leaving aside political considerations, let us return to right and determine the principles that govern this important point. The right which the social compact gives the sovereign over the subjects does not, as I have said, go beyond the limits of public utility. The subjects, therefore, do not have to account to the sovereign for their opinions, except to the extent that these opinions are of importance to the community. For it is of great importance to the state that each citizen have a religion that causes him to love his duties. But the dogmas of that religion are of no interest either to the state or its members, except to the extent that these dogmas relate to morality and to the duties which the one who professes them is bound to fulfill toward others. Each man can have in addition such opinions as he pleases, without it being any of the sovereign's business to know what they are. For since the other world is outside the province of the sovereign, whatever the fate of subjects in the life to come, it is none of its business, so long as they are good citizens in this life.

There is, therefore, a purely civil profession of faith, the articles of which it belongs to the sovereign to establish, not exactly as dogmas of religion, but as sentiments of sociability, without which it is impossible to be a good citizen or a faithful subject. While not having the ability to obligate anyone to believe them, the sovereign can banish from the state anyone who does not believe them. It can banish him not for being impious but for being unsociable, for being incapable of sincerely loving the laws and justice, and of sacrificing his life, if necessary, for his duty. If, after having publicly acknowledged these same dogmas, a person acts as if he does not believe them, he should be put to death; he has committed the greatest of crimes: he has lied before the laws.

The dogmas of the civil religion ought to be simple, few in number, precisely worded, without explanations or commentaries. The existence of a powerful, intelligent, beneficent divinity that foresees and provides; the life to come; the happiness of the just; the punishment of the wicked; the sanctity of the social contract and of the laws. These are the positive dogmas. As for the negative dogmas, I am limiting them to just one, namely intolerance. It is part of the cults we have excluded.

Those who distinguish between civil and theological intolerance are mistaken, in my opinion. Those two types of intolerance are inseparable. It is impossible to live in peace with those one believes to be damned. To love them would be to hate God who punishes them. It is absolutely necessary either to reclaim them or torment them. Whenever theological intolerance is allowed, it is impossible for it not to have some civil effect; and once it does, the sovereign no longer is sovereign, not even over temporal affairs. Thenceforward, priests are the true masters; kings are simply their officers.

Now that there no longer is and never again can be an exclusive national religion, tolerance should be shown to all those that tolerate others, so long as their dogmas contain nothing contrary to the duties of a citizen. But whoever dares to say *outside the church there is no salvation* ought to be expelled from the state, unless the state is the church and the prince is the pontiff. Such a dogma is good only in a theocratic government; in all other forms of government it is ruinous. The reason why Henry IV is said to have embraced the Roman religion should make every decent man, and above all any prince who knows how to reason, leave it.

B2   Jonathan Wolff, 'Who should rule?'

From J. Wolff (1996) *An Introduction to Political Philosophy*, Oxford University Press, pp.85–99.

Rousseau and the general will

> If children are brought up in common in the bosom of equality; if they are imbued with the laws of the state and the precepts of the general will; if they are taught to respect these above all things; if they are surrounded by examples and objects which constantly remind them of the tender mother who nourishes them, of the love she bears them, of the inestimable benefits they receive from her, and of the return they owe her, we cannot doubt that they will learn to cherish one another mutually as brothers, to will nothing contrary to the will of society, to substitute the actions of men and citizens for the futile and vain babbling of sophists, and to become in time defenders and fathers of the country of which they will have been so long the children.
>
> (*Rousseau,* Discourse on Political Economy, *149)*

Plato ... argues that ruling requires a special training or education. Rousseau does not doubt this, but he denies that it is a training that ought to be given only to the few. Far better if everyone acquires the appropriate skills, and then takes an active – democratic – role as part of the 'Sovereign' (the term Rousseau uses for the body of citizens acting collectively, with authority over themselves). A democratic state should therefore place a high value on the education of the citizen.

Rousseau's citizens, then, are to be trained to 'will nothing contrary to the will of society'. This is essential to the health and preservation of the state. Citizenship, for Rousseau, also implies active public service: 'As soon as public service ceases to be the chief business of the citizens, and they would rather serve with their money than with their persons, the state is not far from its fall' (*Social Contract*, bk. III, ch. 15, p.265).

Together with public service, Rousseau requires his citizens to play an active role in political decision-making. By means of a form of direct democracy, all citizens have a hand in the creation of legislation. However, this claim needs to be made out with some care, for there are passages in which Rousseau seems to argue against democracy.

> If we take the term in the strict sense, there never has been a real democracy, and there never will be. It is against the natural order for the many to govern and the few to be governed. It is unimaginable that the people should remain continually assembled to devote their time to public affairs, and it is clear that they cannot set up commissions for that purpose without the form of administration being changed.
>
> *(Social Contract,* bk. III, ch. 4, p.239)

Thus, Rousseau concludes, 'were there a people of gods, their government would be democratic. So perfect a government is not for men' (*Social Contract*, bk. III, ch. 4, p.240).

How should we understand Rousseau's position? We should start with the difficult concept of the general will. First, Rousseau distinguishes the will of all – the product of every individual's particular will – from the general will. Recall the earlier distinction between voting in one's interests, and voting on what one thinks is right. Exercising your vote in the first way – in your interests – is to pursue your particular will. Voting for what is in your view the morally correct outcome, or the common good, is, for Rousseau, a matter of voting in accordance with your idea of the general will.

So what is the general will? A helpful illustration is this: suppose a company has 1,000 employees, and a fixed sum of £1 million available for wage increases. It is in each individual's interests to get as much of this money as possible, so, at the limit, we could say the particular will of each individual is to try to gain an extra £1 million. Adding these particular wills together we get the will of all: a demand for £1,000 million, which, of course, was not on offer. But suppose the employees are represented by a trade union, which acts equally in the interests of all of its members. The union can do nothing except put in a claim for the £1 million, and then share it out equally between all of its members, giving them £1,000 each. This result represents the general will: the policy equally in the interests of all the members. This is not in anyone's special interests, although it is in the common interest. Hence we see an illustration of the difference between the particular wills of all the citizens, and the general will. The general will demands the policy which is equally in everyone's interests. Thus we can think of the general will as the general interest.

Rousseau also claims that the general will must be 'general in its object as well as its essence' (*The Social Contract*, bk. II, ch. 4, p.205). That is, it must apply equally to all citizens. By this Rousseau means that the general will must only make laws which, in principle at least, affect all the citizens, rather than executive orders targeted at particular individuals or groups. We should be ruled by laws, not rulers. The point of this, for Rousseau, is to ensure that the general will expresses a common interest. Under these circumstances, Rousseau thinks, no one has any reason to vote for an oppressive or unnecessary law, for each person is equally affected by all laws. The people, as Sovereign, make laws expressive of the general will.

How, then, are the laws to be applied? After all, they will often require action that singles out groups or even individuals. Legal punishment is the most obvious example. Rousseau's answer is that application of the laws is not the business of the Sovereign, but of the executive or government. The executive arranges day-to-day administration, and Rousseau's view is that it would be absurd to organize this task democratically, in the sense of involving universal active participation. An 'elected aristocracy' – a different sort of democracy, we might think – seems to be Rousseau's preferred arrangement, where the 'wisest should govern the many, where it is assured that they will govern for (the many's) profit, and not for its own' (*Social Contract*, bk. III, ch. 5, p.242).

Note how Rousseau's system differs from Plato's. Even though Rousseau describes his scheme as one in which the wisest govern the many, it is important to remember how restricted a role the government or administration has. The government does not make laws, but only applies or administers them. This is not quite as trivial as it sounds: the government, for example, has the right to declare war. This is a particular act – it names a particular object – and so the people as Sovereign cannot legislate on the matter. All they can do is lay down the general conditions under which war may be declared. It is then for the government to decide whether the conditions are met, and to take the appropriate action. So the key contrast between Plato's philosopher–kings and Rousseau's elective aristocracy is that Rousseau's rulers do not have the power to make laws.

So how are the laws made? Rousseau argues that the 'Sovereign cannot act save when the people is assembled' (*Social Contract*, bk. III, ch. 12, p.261). This is how his system differs from those of contemporary democracies. For laws are made, not in parliament, but at popular assemblies. It is at such assemblies that the general will is discovered:

> When in popular assembly a law is proposed, what the people is asked is not exactly whether it approves or rejects the proposal, but whether it is in conformity with the general will, which is their will. Each man, in giving his vote, states his opinion on that point; and the general will is found by counting votes. When therefore the opinion that is contrary to my own prevails, this proves neither more or less than that I was mistaken, and that what I thought to be the general will was not so.
>
> (*Social Contract,* bk. IV, ch. 2, p.278)

Of course there are a number of objections to Rousseau's proposal. We might be particularly sceptical about the possibility of 'assembling the people'. But before considering these difficulties let us return to the reason why we began to look at Rousseau's position in the first place. The point was that Condorcet had demonstrated that there are conditions under which voting is an extremely good device for finding out the truth about a certain matter. If we assume that people have a better than even chance, on average, of being right, then a majority decision is very likely to get to the right answer, at least in a reasonably large electorate. But, to re-emphasize the necessary conditions for this account to apply, we have first to be sure that people are voting on their idea of the right solution – and not simply for the outcome that most favours them – and that the people do indeed, on average, have a better than even chance of being right. We introduced Rousseau as someone who had intuitively grasped the importance of these conditions, and had outlined a system which met them. Now we should examine whether this system really does so.

First, what justifies the assumption that, if the people are voting on the basis of their view of the general interest, they are likely to be right? Part of the answer must be our original observation that education was as important for Rousseau as it was for Plato. Individuals need to be educated into citizenship. But it is also vital that Rousseau wants to arrange political society in such a way that perceiving the general will should not be difficult, provided, at least, that one's vision is not clouded by particular interests. The common interest is the same for all individuals, and all are equally affected by all the laws passed.

But, we might say, how can this be? Some are rich, some are poor. Some are employers, some are employees. How can it be that everyone is equally affected by the law? Class differences surely lead to distinct, even opposed, interests. The fact that laws single no one out is hardly enough to show that all will be treated in the same way by the law. This gives rise to two lines of scepticism. Why should we think there is a general will at all – a policy that affects everyone equally? Second, even if there is one, it is unlikely to be easy to determine what it is.

Rousseau anticipated both these difficulties, and he has a radical solution to them. If his system is to be practicable, he asserts, then large inequalities must be absent. 'No citizen shall ever be rich enough to buy another, and none poor enough to be forced to sell himself' (*Social Contract*, bk. II, ch. 11, p.225). If class differences make the formation of a general will impossible, then classes must be eliminated. All should stand on an equal footing. At the very least, no one should be so rich as to be able to purchase other people's votes, nor so poor as to be tempted to sell their own. Rousseau does not dwell on the details of how such equality is to be achieved and maintained, but it is clear that a classless society has great advantages from the point of view of democracy. It will be much more likely that everyone will be affected in the same way by the same law, and, further, the complexities of finding out what the best law is are much reduced. Rousseau, of course, accepts that even some people acting in good faith will make errors, but 'the pluses and minuses … cancel one another, and the general will remains as the sum of the differences' (*Social Contract*, bk. II, ch. 3, p.203).

Even though the people meet regularly, they will not be called upon very often to make decisions. A good state needs to pass few laws. Therefore the people can use all their powers to inform themselves of what is required in the cases where they are called upon to vote.

The greatest obstacle to the emergence of the general will that Rousseau sees is not individuals' failure to perceive it, but their failure to be sufficiently motivated to act upon it. The difficulty is felt most keenly 'when intrigues and partial associations are formed at the expenses of the great association' (*Social Contract*, bk. II, ch.3, p.203).

To see this, let us return to the example which we used to illustrate the distinction between the general will and the will of all. We imagined a sum of £1 million, to be divided between 1,000 employees. If these employees were represented by a single trade union then, assuming that there are no reasons for favouring one employee above another, the union would simply put in a request that the money should be split equally, and each should get £1,000. But suppose now that instead of one trade union there are ten, each representing 100 workers. Each of these unions would, no doubt, put in a claim for more than their 'fair share'. Membership of such a union would, in Rousseau's terms, distort one's vision. An individual would be liable to be swayed by spurious arguments 'demonstrating' why members of one's own union should get more. As Rousseau would put it, each of these unions would have a general will in respect to its members, but a particular will with respect to the whole. When 'interest groups' form, and people vote for the interest of their particular group, then there is no reason to believe that the general will would emerge from the process of voting.

Rousseau's main response to this is to recommend that either there should be no political parties, or factions, or, if there are any, there should be very many. In this way the interests of particular groups should have little influence on the decisions of the whole.

Nevertheless, this still does not do enough to explain why citizens will vote for the general will, rather than for their own particular interest. Rousseau's main solution to this problem is that individuals must be made to identify very strongly with the group as a whole. He has a number of devices to ensure this. The most obvious of these devices we have already encountered: education for civic virtue. People need to be brought up the right way so that they learn to 'cherish one another as brothers'. This cements the social bond and widens each person's view so they take an interest in the state as a whole, and hence will naturally seek to advance the general will.

We might think that this is a somewhat sinister idea: it smacks of indoctrination, despite Rousseau's obsession with the protection of the freedom of the individual and some critics claim to have noticed fascistic or totalitarian overtones in Rousseau's thinking. People are to be moulded by education to forget themselves in favour of the state. There are two things to be said in reply to this criticism. First, Rousseau assumes that there should already be bonds of custom and tradition uniting a people before it is fit to receive laws. So education is a way of formalizing and consolidating links which are already present in a community, rather than of imposing an artificial order on a diverse group of people. Second, Rousseau would not be unduly concerned to hear that some of the measures he advocates are not to the taste of modern liberals. This is even more clear in the other two devices he advocates to ensure social unity: 'censorship' and 'civil religion'.

Rousseau supposes that the state needs an 'official censor' whose role is to encourage people to act in accordance with popular morality. Rousseau does not discuss censorship in its modern sense of the suppression of speech or images, although no doubt this would be included within the censor's role. Rousseau's main concern is with enforcing and discouraging types of behaviour. In essence, the job of the censor is to ridicule, and so discourage, certain forms of anti-social behaviour. As an example, Rousseau tells us, 'Certain drunkards from Samos polluted the tribunal of the Ephors: the next day, a public edict gave Samians permission to be filthy. An actual punishment would not have been so severe an impunity' (*Social Contract*, bk. IV, ch.8, p.298). By such means the censor is charged with the duty of upholding, and clarifying where necessary, public morality.

As a final device to ensure social unity, Rousseau proposes that each state should be regulated by what he calls a 'civil religion'. In brief, there are three parts to Rousseau's account of religion. First, he requires that every citizen should subscribe to some religion or other, for this will 'make him love his duty'. Second, a diversity of religions should be tolerated, but only those which themselves include a principle of toleration. Otherwise some citizens will be compelled to become enemies, which is contrary to the idea of social peace. Finally, and most distinctively, in addition to private morality, each person should subscribe to the civil religion. This should have articles which are 'not exactly … religious dogmas, but … social sentiments without which a man cannot be a good citizen or a faithful subject' (*Social Contract*, bk. IV, ch.8, p.307).

In sum then, if Rousseau's system were in existence it would seem to have a good chance of meeting the two conditions we have set down for Condorcet's argument to apply. The conditions were that people had to vote on moral grounds, rather than in their own self-interest, and to have, on average, a better than even chance of getting the morally right answer. In Rousseau's ideal state it is plausible that these conditions will be met. Of course, it does not follow that observing Rousseau's proposals is the only way in which the conditions can be satisfied: perhaps we could devise an alternative system. But let us concentrate on Rousseau. Even if we concede that his system meets Condorcet's conditions, is it a system we should adopt?

Freedom and equality

To recall the earlier discussion, we noted, in essence, two types of response to Plato. One was to argue that democracy, in principle, is a way of achieving the 'right result' that is at least as good as, or better than, rule by experts. This instrumental form of justification, as we called it, corresponds to the argument of Rousseau we have just considered. The second type of response was to consider the intrinsic value of democracy. In essence, we can see this as the question of how well democracy expresses or advances the values of freedom and equality. Discussion of this question will have the further advantage of helping us to decide whether Rousseau's system is one which we should wish to put into practice.

First, then, how expressive of the idea of equality is Rousseau's polity? One way in which equality entered the argument was through the idea that, without rough equality of wealth, factions would form. This would not only cloud the judgement of the voters, but perhaps create an obstacle to the existence of a general will: a policy equally in the interests of all voters. For the rich would seek a set of laws which particularly benefited them, and would have the money and influence to arrange things in their own favour. So, as we noted, Rousseau assumes that genuine democracy presupposes a classless society.

The idea of the general will itself, however, is even more strongly egalitarian. The correct policy is one which benefits all citizens equally. On the face of it, then, it would be hard to devise a system which gives a greater weight to equality, particularly when combined with the democratic principle that all citizens have an equal say in the attempt to determine the nature of the general will on any given case.

Unfortunately, the appearance of equality within Rousseau's system is somewhat misleading. Rousseau always uses the masculine form to refer to the citizens. This is no accident of language. Rousseau believed that women were subordinate beings, and he simply seems to have assumed that the privilege of citizenship should be extended only to men. Thus the doctrine of the equality of citizens is rather soured by Rousseau's assumption that there would naturally be inequalities between male citizens and female non-citizens.

This inconsistency in Rousseau's system was addressed by perhaps the first major advocate of women's rights, Mary Wollstonecraft, in her *Vindication of the Rights of Women*, published in 1792. Wollstonecraft argued that there was no basis for the exclusion of women from the citizenry. But even she had a blind spot. The emancipated female citizen is assumed to have female domestic servants, and the idea that such servants should also have the vote is something which Wollstonecraft seems simply to have ignored. It was generally assumed, until relatively recently, that the only people entitled to vote were those with some property stake in the country. Those without property could not be trusted to use their votes 'responsibly'.

However, a motivation also moving Wollstonecraft, Rousseau, and, indeed, the Ancient Greeks, is the more mundane thought that those people who are active as citizens do not have the time to wash their own clothes or cook their own food. To perform one's duty as an active citizen is time-consuming, if one is both to keep oneself well informed, and attend the public forum or assembly. Anyone engaged in public life needs domestic support staff. The Greeks took for granted that democracy was consistent with slavery, Rousseau that it was consistent with sexual inequality, and Wollstonecraft that it was consistent with the disfranchisement of the poor. Two things have brought about the changes which have made universal suffrage possible. One is the (rather depressing) view that a right to vote does not bring with it an onerous responsibility to keep oneself well informed about political and economic matters; the other that in the developed world at least, household machinery has greatly eased the burdens of domestic work. It might be an exaggeration to say that the washing machine has made democracy possible, but it has certainly helped.

However, despite Rousseau's exclusion of women from the franchise, the real logic of his political thought implies that there is no good reason for this exclusion. We can, then, construct a model of genuine equality on the basis of Rousseau's proposals.

So much for equality. How about freedom? It is not difficult to detect significant limitations of freedom in Rousseau's chosen polity. The central restriction is simply the other side of the coin to the creation of the social bond. Freedom of thought is severely restricted, particularly in the area of religion. First, atheism is barred. Second, intolerant religions are not to be tolerated. Third, all must affirm the civil religion. And woe betide the hypocrite: 'If any one, after publicly recognising these dogmas (of civil religion), behaves as if he does not believe them, let him be punished by death: he has committed the worst of all crimes, that of lying before the law' (*Social Contract*, bk. IV, ch.8, p.307). When we add to this the existence of the office of the censor, whose role it is to enforce public or customary morality, then individuals appear to lose any freedom to be unconventional ...

With this restrictive illiberal background in mind, we may ask how Rousseau can maintain that he solved the problem of finding a form of association in which 'while uniting himself with all (each associate) may still obey himself alone, and remain as free as before' (*Social Contract*, bk. I, ch.6, p.191).

The answer is that Rousseau holds what has been called a 'positive' notion of freedom ... the thought is that freedom is not simply a matter of being able to follow your desires, unconstrained by others (a 'negative' notion) but instead something which requires certain types of action. Typically, theorists of positive freedom define freedom in terms of 'living the life that the rational person would choose to live'. In Rousseau's case such a life – the rational life – is available only in civil society. 'The mere impulse of appetite is slavery, while obedience to a law we prescribe to ourselves is liberty' (*Social Contract*, bk. IV, ch. 8, p.196). The way, of course, in which we prescribe laws to ourselves is through voting as a member of the Sovereign. It is only by acting in accordance with the laws created by the Sovereign – acting on the general will – that we can be said, according to Rousseau, to be truly free.

It has been pointed out by critics that on this view one can be 'forced to be free'; in fact this is a phrase that Rousseau himself uses. Consider the case of someone who believes that the general will requires one policy (policy A), while the majority adopt another (policy B). Policy B, let us suppose, represents the general will. In that case our person will be forced to act according to policy B, and as freedom is identified with acting on the general will, then it follows that the person has been forced to be free. Rousseau would say that anything else – doing what one prefers, for example – is slavery to one's impulses, and not true freedom. Opponents of Rousseau have pointed out that on this basis even highly repressive regimes can be defended on grounds of their support of freedom. So even though we can rescue Rousseau's system from inequality, it is very unclear whether we can say – as Rousseau so wants us to say – that it advances the value of freedom.

Radical criticism of Rousseau

This criticism has been taken up and extended by certain contemporary writers, who, while being strongly influenced by Rousseau's writing, feel his ideal of the state needs to be improved and repaired in a number of ways. There are three, closely related, criticisms to be made.

The first focuses on the idea of the general will. Even if it is true that in a closely unified, highly equal society a general will can be formed and relatively easily perceived, it is not true that contemporary societies conform to this ideal; nor is it desirable that they should. Economic class is not the only obstacle to the formation of a general will; we also belong to different religions, have different moral and philosophical ideas, and come from differing cultural, ethnic, and racial backgrounds. Now this does not mean that there can never be a policy equally in the interests of all: despite our differences we all have similar basic needs. But beyond this, the fact that we value different things – economic progress or the protection of the natural environment, for example – can lead to conflict. Thus on many issues it is very unlikely that there could be any policy that is equally in the interests of all. Or, if there were, that it would be easy to discover. Perhaps then, we must simply drop Rousseau's key assumption that citizens can form their wills into a general will.

Secondly, Rousseau's treatment of those who hold a minority view is hard to admire. Dissenters are to be 'forced to be free'. Those who first affirm the principles of the civil religion and then disobey them are to be put to death. Against the background of the tight unity of the state, dissent is a crime, and crime is treason. This might be marginally defensible if the majority were always right about the general will, and dissenters therefore either mistaken or anti-social. But if there is no general will, then this argument is appalling in more than one sense.

Finally, Rousseau's critics do not accept that freedom should be equated with obedience, even 'obedience to a law one makes for oneself'. Or, to put this another way, within Rousseau's system 'making the law for oneself' is simply a matter of having some say in the decision-making procedure. But suppose, again, one is in the minority, and one's views do not become law. Then, while it may be justified to coerce such people to obey the law, it seems outrageous to say that such coercion makes them 'free', that they are being brought to obey a law that they have created for themselves. Even though the minority have taken part in the decision-making procedure, the law has been created despite them, not because of them.

The force of these criticisms can now be seen. In order for Rousseau to be able to argue that democracy is instrumentally justified – that it is a highly reliable way of achieving morally correct outcomes – he has to draw the bonds of social unity very tight. So tight, in fact, that the system becomes unacceptably repressive. So the same measures which, in Rousseau's model, make democracy defensible in instrumental terms also make it intrinsically undesirable. In an amended form it may achieve equality, but not freedom as we recognize it, nor pluralism, nor diversity. The price we have to pay for the general will is too high.

Thus Rousseau's system needs repair. And, indeed, in the light of these criticisms we can point to another oddity in Rousseau's ideal polity – an oddity which has gone unremarked so far in this discussion. This is the extent to which Rousseau allows genuine political participation. Although Rousseau's citizens are regularly called upon to vote, somewhat paradoxically he seems to discourage them from taking too active a role in politics. First, as we saw, he does not advocate a democratic assembly, and second, the assumption that only clouded perception stands in the way of unanimity leads Rousseau to conclude that 'long debates, dissensions and tumult proclaim the ascendancy of particular interests and the decline of the state' (*Social Contract*, bk. IV, ch.2, p.276).

However, once we drop the assumption that we can regularly and easily perceive a general will – in fact, if we drop the assumption that there is a general will altogether – then politics takes on a new cast. There now seems an urgent need to hear all voices, all arguments, and all positions. Voters can still be represented as aiming at 'the best' for the community. But perhaps what 'the best' is in any case can be a highly contested matter. Furthermore, it will probably be very controversial which policies would be most likely to achieve it.

Thus Rousseau's critics have argued that extensive political debate is not a sign of decay, but vital to the functioning of democratic politics. Furthermore, outvoted minorities have no duty to change their mind about what is correct. In general we would expect them to obey the law, but they can continue to speak up, and, if they feel strongly enough, to agitate for change. Perhaps civil disobedience can also be justified on democratic grounds. If you sincerely believe that a wrong decision has been made by the majority, then you may have not only a right but a duty to draw attention to this, by whatever means necessary. Treating conscientious disobedience as treason, in order to preserve social unity, is surely a mistake. The dissenting citizen has a place. He or she should not be silenced for the sake of peace: perhaps the majority is wrong. But even if the majority is right, attention should still be paid to dissenters.

Section C ART HISTORY: DAVID AND FRIEDRICH

C1 Robert Herbert, extract from *David, Voltaire, 'Brutus' and the French Revolution*

From R.L. Herbert (1972) *David, Voltaire, 'Brutus' and the French Revolution: An Essay in Art and Politics*, Harmondsworth, Penguin, pp.16–17.

The story of Lucius Junius Brutus, who lived five hundred years before Caesar's assassin Marcus Brutus, begins with the rise to power of the last king of Rome, Tarquin the Proud. Tarquin and his wife Tullia had murdered their first mates to be free to marry one another, and then Tarquin killed the king, his new wife's father. The usurper put many senators to death and ruled autocratically. He also murdered most of the family of Brutus, his nephew, who survived in the royal household by feigning stupidity (brutishness – hence the name Brutus).

This dissolute monarchy came to an end when Tarquin's son Sextus raped the virtuous Lucretia, the wife of Collatinus. She called together her father and her husband, who came accompanied by Publius Valerius and Brutus, and stabbed herself in their presence to expiate the stain. Brutus suddenly revealed his true nature by drawing the knife from the fatal wound and swearing on Lucretia's blood to rid Rome of the Tarquins and of the very institution of monarchy. He then had the other three men swear the same oath over the knife, and later in public bound the populace to it as well. Brutus then led the successful fight against Tarquin, and the royal family was exiled. The first Roman republic was established (508 B.C.) with Brutus and Collatinus elected co-consuls. It is at this point that Livy began his Book II (Baker edition) with the memorable words 'Henceforward I am to treat of the affairs, civil and military, of a free people, for such the Romans were now become; of annual magistrates, and the authority of the laws exalted above that of man.'

These events would undoubtedly have sufficed to give Brutus adequate fame, but he performed another act so terrifying in its devotion to the state that it became the central element of his legend. His two adolescent sons, Titus and Tiberius, were drawn into a royalist conspiracy by their mother's family, the Vitelii, and Brutus was obliged to order and to witness their execution. Livy merely comments that at the execution 'the looks and countenance of Brutus afforded an extraordinary spectacle, the feelings of the father often struggling with the character of the magistrate', but Plutarch (Clough/Dryden edition) was more disturbed.

'Brutus ... is said not to have turned aside his face, nor allowed the least glance of pity to soften and smooth his aspect of rigor and austerity, but sternly watched his children suffer ... An action truly open alike to the highest commendation and the strongest censure; for either the greatness of his virtue raised him above the impressions of sorrow, or the extravagance of his misery took away all sense of it; but neither seemed common, or the result of humanity, but either divine or brutish.'

C2 Charles Étienne Gabriel Cuvillier,[1] Letter to Joseph Vien,[2] 10 August 1789

From R.L. Herbert (1972) *David, Voltaire, 'Brutus' and the French Revolution: An Essay in Art and Politics*, Harmondsworth, Penguin, pp.124–5, translated by R.L. Herbert, footnotes edited.

Versailles, 10 August 1789

At our last meeting, Monsieur, about the coming opening of the Salon, the idea of which preoccupies Monsieur the General Director[3] almost as much as making use of the waters, I expressed to you the justified and entire confidence he places in the prudence and caution of the Academy in organizing this Salon. I will not repeat here the reasons and the motives that unhesitatingly determine Monsieur the General Director to deprive neither the capital nor the artists of an event interesting for the pleasures of the former, valuable for the glory of the latter, and which, in the present moment, can serve morale as a useful diversion. None of that will have escaped your notice and will be equally understood by Messieurs of the Academy, hence it is only in a certain measure to complete the instructions prepared by Monsieur the General Director that I will offer a few observations here.

Monsieur the General Director thinks that one could not exercise too much caution in the choice of subjects which will be exhibited, relative to the interpretations which might escape from an observer and which could be awakened by others. The theatre provides us each day with the most unexpected examples.[4] I only feel all the more how difficult it is to predict all that might be imagined, and my unique aim is to urge the committee to use all possible precaution.

The heading of portraits lets one more readily put oneself on guard, because in general the sitters being known, one is in the position of measuring public opinion and of not risking anything; I imagine that concerning this, M. Lavoisier[5] will be the first to wish not to show his portrait. It is not that he could in any sense be ranked among those whom one could think badly of, but one can let him judge that. On the subject of portraits I am inclined to fear that Monsieur de Tollendal might renew the project of exhibiting this terrifying painting which it was so difficult to set aside in 1787;[6] but, at the same time, I am reassured by the very virtue of Monsieur de Tollendal and by the loftiness of his views which will let him see at a glance the danger of furnishing more food to the fermentation. It is in this regard that I am comforted, as much as I could be, by learning that Monsieur David's painting is still far from finished; and, à propos this artist, I think as you, Monsieur, that his painting of *Paris and Helen*[7] can be exhibited without remaining fears, by suppressing the owner's name. In this the only concern I see is the glory of the Academy and that of the artist.

I ought to express very particularly to you, Monsieur, the really deep distress which Monsieur the General Director would feel at the decision some of the artists might take not to contribute to the exhibition, and Monsieur the General Director urges you to press them on his behalf not to follow that course. In case there were too much empty space, the precise wish of Monsieur the General Director is that it be occupied by paintings sent to previous exhibitions that were not seen, or poorly seen. Messieurs *Roslin*[8] and *Durameau*[9] are in a position to respond to both cases, and I rely on them to be ready for the next committee meeting. I have the honor, etc.

Cuvillier

P.S. – Will you permit me to make the personal observation that it will perhaps be well to arrange the pictures so that the little ones will not be within reach of certain hands?

[1] Charles-Étienne-Gabriel Cuvillier, of the Royal Fine Arts office.

[2] Joseph Vien, President of the Royal Academy of Painting and Sculpture.

[3] The Count d'Angiviller, General Director of Fine Arts.

[4] Cuvillier may have been thinking of the recent fuss over censorship of Chénier's play, *Charles IX*. This play told the story of the sixteenth-century Catholic monarch who had allowed various members of his court, including his mother, Catherine of Medici, to carry out the famous St Bartholomew's Day massacre of Protestants. Royalist theatre committees had refused to let Chénier's play be performed in the National Theatre in Paris, for fear that audiences would draw unfortunate parallels with the existing French court. Chénier replied by making a plea for freedom of speech and expression in a pamphlet entitled *De la liberté du théâtre en France* (*On the Freedom of French Theatre*) written in June 1789. He argued that censorship of this kind was not only unnecessary (Charles IX had died a long time ago) but was also inappropriate for a nation which wanted to be 'free' and 'enlightened'. A war of pamphleteering and the imposition and lifting of a series of bans ensued, the play eventually being presented for the first time on November 4th 1789. The audience did indeed draw parallels with the eighteenth-century French monarchy.

[5] The reference is to David's portrait of *Lavoisier and his Wife* (Plate 130). Lavoisier, a noble, scientist, Commissioner of Gunpowder and tax collector, was regarded as a controversial figure because he belonged to the reformist '89 club, had been involved in collating the grievances of the inhabitants of Blois in a *cahier de doléances* (book of grievances) in March 1789; and had sponsored proposals in favour of restraining royal power. As Commissioner of Gunpowder, Lavoisier was feared by all sides. Robert Herbert resumes the story: 'The suggested exclusion of Lavoisier's portrait was because of a violent incident that took place just four days before Cuvillier wrote to Vien. Lavoisier had ordered the removal from Paris of the stock of old, low grade powder, to make way for new. It was loaded on boats but seized by the people of the district. They feared Tarquin-like plots on all sides, and were convinced that the powder was being sent to aristocratic emigrés. On 6 August, Lavoisier was nearly hung by an angry mob, and only vindicated himself at the last moment. The clamor did not die down for several weeks, so Cuvillier had good reason to fear controversy if Lavoisier's portrait was exhibited.' (Herbert, 1972, p.59)

[6] The painting in question is Jean Baptiste Claude Robin's *Trophime Girard, Marquis de Lally-Tollendal Unveiling the Bust of his Father (Plate 131)*. It had been excluded from the Salon of 1787 but was eventually included, at Tollendal's insistence, in the Salon of 1789. Lally-Tollendal's father had been charged with treason after leading the French into war against the British in India and suffering an honourable defeat. He had been imprisoned in the Bastille and beheaded in 1766. His son tried to restore his father's reputation and in 1778 Louis XVI acknowledged that the name of Lally-Tollendal's father had been unjustly blemished. The painting shows the son unveiling a bust of his father with one hand while holding his petition to the king ("Sire, my father was not guilty") in the other. Lally-Tollendal was not anti-monarchist: on 5th August 1789, he had called the king, "Restorer of French Liberty". But Cuvillier might have feared that the subject of Robin's painting would incite suspicion of royal treachery and injustice.

[7] A painting by David (Colour Plate 42) commissioned by the comte d'Artois, the king's brother, and intended for exhibition at the Salon of 1789. (It never actually appeared there.) The Count had a reputation as a rake and a libertine. His name was dropped from the Salon catalogue: it might have prompted thoughts of dissolute monarchy. This painting on the theme of sexual love and conquest is discussed in TV12.

[8] Alexandre Roslin (1718–93): a Swedish portrait painter who worked a lot in Paris.

[9] Louis-Jean-Jacques Durameau (1733–96): painter of history and genre subjects who also worked on the ceiling of the Galérie d'Apollon in the Louvre.

C3 Anita Brookner, extract from *Jacques-Louis David*

From A. Brookner (1980) *Jacques-Louis David*, Chatto & Windus, pp.112–13, footnotes added.

Marat was a complicated character who began his career as a doctor, with degrees from the universities of Bordeaux and St. Andrew's. In 1777 he was appointed physician to the troops of the king's brother, the comte d'Artois (for whom David painted *Paris and Helen*) and he was in great demand as a court doctor. In 1786 he resigned his appointment, and two years later came to the notice of the public as a journalist. From 1788 to 1792 he edited a newspaper entitled *L'Ami du Peuple*,[1] in September 1792 the name was changed to *Journal de la République française*,[2] but Marat retained the sobriquet of 'the people's friend'. This journal specialized in denunciation. Marat was undoubtedly paranoid and was famous for his battle-cry, 'Nous sommes trahis!'.[3] He was a red revolutionary with no Antique polish; he approved of the death penalty; he insisted upon it. His are the archetypal voice and personality of the Terror. He had also supported David in the latter's struggle against the Académie ... Marat was an ugly man. He suffered from a skin disease which is referred to in contemporary accounts as 'une lèpre',[4] and the irritation was so severe that he was obliged to immerse himself as frequently as possible in cool water ... Marat was hated, feared and dangerous.

The scene now shifts to Caen, where citizeness Marie-Anne-Charlotte Corday, after reading her Plutarch,[5] made up her mind to assassinate the friend of the people. On 23 April 1793 she obtained a passport for Paris, giving as the pretext for her visit a need to consult someone at the Ministry of the Interior on behalf of a friend. On 11 July she arrived in Paris. She asked at the stage coach office for the name of an hôtel and was directed to the Hôtel de la Providence, 19 Rue des Vieux Augustins, where a servant told her that Marat had been ill and was confined to his apartment in the Rue des Cordeliers. This was bad news, for she had intended to stab him in the National Convention. On Saturday 13 July she bought a kitchen knife with a long blade from Badin, in the arcades of the former Palais-Royal. She took a cab to Marat's house, where his mistress Simone Evrard refused to admit her. She returned to her hotel at noon and wrote a letter to Marat promising to reveal details of plots in Caen and in the Vendée, this of course being precisely the sort of thing that Marat liked to denounce. She posted her letter and waited in her room for an answer. To while away the time, she summoned the hairdresser, then changed into a spotted muslin dress with a pink fichu.[6] A tall black hat with a green cockade and black tassels completed her outfit. She wrote another note and put it into her pocket to deliver personally. Into her bodice she put her birth certificate, an address to the French people, and the knife. At seven in the evening she took another cab to Marat's house.

Simone Evrard again refused to admit her but Charlotte Corday took advantage of the arrival of a newspaper seller and a printer to slip into the apartment. Marat, who was in his bath, sheeted to prevent the scaly sores on his body from coming into contact with the copper lining of the wooden tub, and with a turban soaked in vinegar round his head, overheard angry voices and called out to have Corday admitted. She entered the room, on the wall of which she could have seen two crossed pistols with the legend *La Mort*,[7] took a sheet of paper, and dipped a pen in ink to write the names of the plotters of Caen. She then pulled out the knife and stabbed Marat in the right lung. Marat called out to Simone Evrard, 'A moi, chère amie, à moi',[8] then lost consciousness. His body was lifted from the bath by two members of the household who knocked Charlotte Corday to the floor. She made no attempt to resist. Marat was pronounced dead at a quarter to eight in the evening by a member of the Collège de Médecine who lived on the floor below. Because of the heat of the night and the unhealthy state of Marat's blood, embalming was begun immediately.

[1] The Friend of the People.

[2] Journal of the French Republic.

[3] "We are betrayed!"

[4] Leprosy, plague.

[5] Plutarch (*c.*46–*c.*126 CE) was a Greek essayist whose *Parallel Lives* drew out the moral and political implications of the lives of 23 pairs of Greek and Roman soldiers and statesmen.

[6] Small triangular shawl of lace etc. for the shoulders and neck.

[7] Death.

[8] 'Help me, my love'.

C4 Caspar David Friedrich, statement on *The Tetschen Altar*

From H. Börsch-Supan and H. Joachim Neidhardt (1972) *Caspar David Friedrich 1774–1840: Romantic Landscape Painting in Dresden*, Tate Gallery, p.104, footnotes added.

Description of the Picture. The cross is raised on high at the summit of the rocks, surrounded by evergreen firs. Evergreen ivy is entwined around its stem. The sun sinks with brilliant rays and the Saviour on the cross shines in the crimson of the evening glow.

Description of the Frame. The frame has been constructed according to Herr Friedrich's specifications by the sculptor Kühn. At each side the frame takes the form of a Gothic column. Palm branches[1] rise up from these to make an arch over the picture. Amongst the branches are the heads of five angels, who all look down in adoration onto the cross. Above the middlemost angel the evening star shines in the purest silvery lustre. Below, in a broad inset, the all-seeing eye of God is enclosed by the divine triangle surrounded by rays of light. Ears of corn and vines bow[2] down on either side towards the all-seeing eye, indicating the body of Him who is nailed to the cross.

Interpretation of the Picture. Jesus Christ, nailed to the tree, is turned here towards the sinking sun, the image of the eternal life-giving father. With Jesus' teaching an old world dies – that time when God the Father moved directly on the earth. This sun sank and the earth was not able to grasp the departing light any longer. There shines forth in the gold of the evening light the purest, noblest metal of the Saviour's figure on the cross, which thus reflects on earth in a softened glow. The cross stands erected on a rock, unshakably firm like our faith in Jesus Christ. The firs stand around the evergreen, enduring through all ages, like the hopes of man in Him, the crucified.

[1] In much religious art, a symbol of the Christian victory over death.

[2] Corn and the vine found together in this way usually symbolize the eucharistic elements: bread and wine.

C5 Jacques-Louis David: a chronology

Adapted from A. Brookner (1980) *Jacques-Louis David*, Chatto & Windus, pp.39–50, 51–2, 58–63, 65, 66, 75–6, 86–7, 90, 99, 101, 103, 119, 121–2, 123–135, 139, 146–7, 148–9, 150–54, 175–6, 184–6, 187.

1748	Born in Paris on 30 August.
1764–5	Introduced to Boucher, a painter of popular mythological subjects, by his uncle.
1766	On advice from Boucher became pupil of the Neoclassical artist Vien (see *La Marchande d'Amours*, Plate 146).
1774	Won the Prix de Rome with *Antiochus and Stratonice*. It was his fourth attempt at the Royal Academy prize.
1775	Travelled to Rome with Vien who had been made Director of the French Academy there. Visited Parma, Bologna, Florence, Pompeii and Herculaneum.
1780	Completed *Saint Roch* in Rome. Returned to Paris.
1781	Exhibited successfully at the Salon his *Saint Roch*, portrait of Count Potocki and other works.
1782	Married Charlotte Pécoul, daughter of one of the king's building contractors, and acquired a large dowry.
1783	Exhibited *Andromache Mourning Hector* at the Salon. Admitted to full membership of the Academy on the strength of this painting.
1784–5	Returned to Rome where he painted and exhibited *The Oath of the Horatii* (Colour Plate 43). David advised officials in Paris, where the picture was to appear at the Salon, that the painting was larger than had been commissioned.
1789	Exhibited at the Salon *The Lictors returning to Brutus the Bodies of his Sons* (Colour Plate 41) as well as *The Loves of Paris and Helen* (Colour Plate 42), which he'd painted for the king's brother, the comte d'Artois.
1791	Exhibited at the Salon drawing of *The Oath in the Tennis Court* (Plate 126).
1792	Elected deputy to the National Convention.
1793	Voted for the death of the King. Was named a member of the Committee of General Security. Painted *The Death of Marat* (Colour Plate 46).
1794	Divorced his wife. In June, designed and co-ordinated the Festival of the Supreme Being marking the climax of his revolutionary career. After Robespierre was executed on 28 July, David was denounced and arrested on 2 August.
1795	Painted many portraits. All revolutionary detainees amnestied on 26 October.

1796	Remarried his estranged wife.
1799	Exhibited *The Sabine Women* (Colour Plate 48) at the Louvre and charged an entrance fee. Napoleon Bonaparte's coup d'état, 10 November.
1800	Declined the title of painter to the Government. Completed *Bonaparte Crossing the Alps at Mont Saint Bernard* (Colour Plate 47).
1804	Accepted appointment as First Painter to the Emperor.
1805	Painted the coronation of Napoleon and Josephine.
1815–16	The monarchy restored, David was exiled on the grounds of his regicide sympathies. (He had voted for the death of Louis XVI.) He went to Belgium as it was French-speaking and near to home.
1817–24	Completed works including *Wrath of Achilles* and *Mars Disarmed by Venus*.
1825	Died in Brussels on 29 December and was buried there.

C6 Caspar David Friedrich: a chronology

From W.Vaughan (1980) *German Romantic Painting*, New Haven and London, Yale University Press, pp.65–116.

1774	Born in Greifswald, Pomerania, on the North German coast (see Figure 12.4, Block 3).
1781	Mother died.
1787	His brother drowned while trying to save Friedrich's life.
1790	Apprenticed for four years to Johann Gottfried Quistorp, a drawing master from Greifswald University, who taught Friedrich to draw by using academic copybooks (figure drawings based on the poses and proportions of antique copybooks). Quistorp introduced Friedrich to Ludwig Theobul Kosegarten, a Pomeranian pastor and poet.
1794–8	Studied art at the Copenhagen Academy. Continued study of the antique and copied engravings of old masters. Came into contact with Lorentzen and Juel, landscape artists. Did watercolours of local scenery and coloured prints of drawings of Norwegian mountains.
1798	Began to work in oils. Moved to Dresden, which remained his base for the rest of his life. Came into contact with realist landscape artists influenced by the Dutch seventeenth-century tradition. Began to make careful studies in sketchbooks of plants and trees (see *Plant Study*, Plate 154) many of which showed a neo-classical concern with clarity of line. Added sepia washes to some of his sketches and became more interested in tone.

1805	Awarded joint first prize by Goethe for two sepias at Weimar exhibition.
1808	Exhibited *Cross in the Mountains* (Colour Plate 53).
1810	*Abbey in the Oak Forest* (Colour Plate 58) bought by the Crown Prince of Prussia after it had been exhibited at the Berlin Academy. Elected member of Berlin Academy.
1818	Married Caroline Bommer. Visited Greifswald and Rügen, an island off the Pomeranian coast (see Figure 12.4, Block 3).
1825	Suffered stroke.
1835	A further severe stroke.
1840	Died in Dresden.

ACKNOWLEDGEMENTS

Grateful acknowledgement is made to the following sources for permission to reproduce material in this book:

A3 and A8: Levy, D.G., Applewhite, H.B. and Johnson, M.D. (1979) *Women in Revolutionary Paris, 1789–1795*. Copyright 1979 by the Board and Trustees of the University of Illinois. Used with the permission of the University of Illinois Press;

A4: Wright, D.G. (1974) *Revolution and Terror in France, 1789–1795*, Longman. Reprinted by permission of Addison Wesley Longman Ltd;

A10, A11, A12, A14, A15 and A16: Stewart, J.H. (1951) *A Documentary Survey of the French Revolution*, Simon and Schuster/Prentice Hall;

A20: Hufton, O. (1976) 'Women in revolution, 1789–1796', in D. Johnson (ed.) *French Society and the Revolution*, Cambridge University Press/The Past and Present Society;

A21: From WOMEN, WAR & REVOLUTION, edited by Carol R. Berkin and Clara M. Lovett (New York: Holmes and Meier, 1980). Copyright (c) 1980 by Holmes and Meier Publishers, Inc. Reproduced by the permission of the publisher;

A22: Furet, F. and Richet, D. (1970) in S. Hardman (trans.) *The French Revolution*, Weidenfeld and Nicolson;

A23: Anderson, M.S. (1985) *The Ascendancy of Europe, 1815-1914*, 2nd edn. Reprinted by permission of Addison Wesley Longman Ltd;

B1: Rousseau, J.J. in D.A. Cress (trans.) (1987) *The Basic Political Writings*. Copyright © 1987 by Hackett Publishing Company, Inc. All rights reserved;